LET'S USE THE LOCALITY

We shall not cease from exploration
And the end of all our exploring
Will be to arrive where we started
And know the place for the first time.
From Little Gidding 'Four Quartets'
by T. S. Eliot

By the same author

Let's Work Large
Let's Make Pictures
A Dickens Anthology *(with Frank Peacock)*

Plate 1
*Young children looking at 18th-century
houses nestling beneath 20th-century
tower blocks.*

Let's use the locality

A HANDBOOK FOR TEACHERS

HENRY PLUCKROSE
Head of Prior Weston School, Barbican,
London

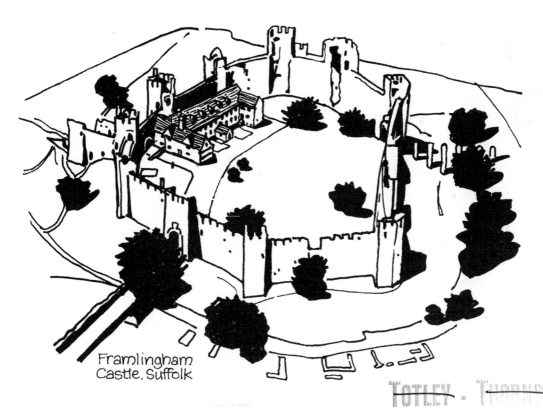

Framlingham
Castle, Suffolk

MILLS & BOON LIMITED London

First published in Great Britain 1971 by
Mills & Boon Limited, 17–19 Foley Street,
London, W1A 1DR

© 1971 Henry Pluckrose

ISBN 0 263.51601.6

Made and printed by Oxley Press Limited
Morrison & Gibb Ltd., Edinburgh

Any orders or enquiries should not be sent
to the printers but to the publishers
(address at top of page).

Contents

Acknowledgements

I would like to record my thanks to the people who have helped me in the presentation of this book.

G. W. Hales for his excellent photographs.

The Dean of Gloucester for permission to include a photograph of ecclesiastical embroidery (Plate 11).

Marvin Lichtner, photographer for Time Life Incorporated, for permission to reproduce Plates 5 and 6.

Mrs Joan Bryant, Mills and Boon Ltd, for her advice during the initial preparation of the manuscript.

Frank Peacock, sometime Headteacher of the John Ruskin Primary School, London, S.E.5, for his helpful comments on the educational content of the manuscript.

Alec Davis, Mills and Boon Ltd for his line drawings.

Bridget Jackson for preparing Appendix 3.

Cicely Tipple for the care she has shown in preparing the typescript.

And finally to all the children I have worked with who have led me to believe, by the enthusiasm they have shown for such things as misericords and dungeons, that this book will be of some use to all who work with young people.

Preface

Of all the changes that I have seen in the education of young children since I started teaching, perhaps the one which has been most far-reaching has been our attempt to give meaning and substance to the curricula.

Now far be it for me to suggest that until Plowden and Newsom children were taught nothing of worth. Of course school programmes have always had content. What has changed is our concept of what the content ought to be. Probably most Edwardian twelve-year-olds knew that Normans lived in castles and that the Tudors used red brick as well as daub and wattle for their fine houses. They knew because they had been told and because their school books said so. Similarly they knew that 5 x 9 always made 45 (without resorting to rods or abacus), that John was not a good king and that Paris was in France.

But bare facts – however well presented – leave us a little cold in an age dominated by the television screen and a mass communications industry the like of which mankind has never known before. Children whose appetites have been whetted by visual journeys beneath the sea, who have seen man stand on the Moon, are hardly likely to remain enthusiastic for a school programme whose trips into the real world are little more than periodic dips into a fading textbook. To-day's children are far more sophisticated, and I think, rather more enquiring than those of even a generation ago. Accepting this, we have had to rethink the ways in which knowledge is presented to children. Flat chunks of information, imparted in instalments, might be enough to get them through this or that examination: it will certainly not make them sensitive

people, giving them a thirst for further information and perhaps the facility for looking and seeing which will remain with them in adulthood to enrich their leisure hours. But if learning is to be based largely on practical experience or "doing" rather than simply sitting and being filled with facts, the teacher's role will need to undergo a radical change.

The aim of this book is to suggest ways in which teachers can use the school locality as the starting point for research and to indicate how the information so obtained can be recorded in pictures, models, maps and plans and in the spoken and written word. The biggest difficulty I have had to overcome has been to present my ideas in such a way as to be meaningful to teachers working in utterly different parts of the country. The teacher working in a new town has (at first glance) far less around him to draw upon than the teacher whose school is in the centre of Salisbury; the teacher in rural Framlingham far more than the teacher whose school is hidden in a Yorkshire dale.

And yet, when one really begins to look for evidence of man upon his environment, it is surprising what one can discover. The houses that the children are living in, the roadway that runs past the school, the local shop, the school itself, all illustrate to some degree our history and the struggles of the long-since-dead to master the environment — to cut down trees and grow crops, to quarry stone and build, to fashion clay and iron, reed and willow, to construct boats and barges, mills and factories.

I have also tried to provide a simple county by county gazetteer (Appendix 1)

for teachers who happen to be passing
through an area with a group of children
and who want an interesting place to stop
to break the journey. (I'm thinking particularly
of school journey parties travelling by coach
from one centre to another.) This section,
however, should also prove of use to teachers
new to an area and who would like some
starting points for environmental studies.

It has been, of course, impossible to include
every church of note or every old building of
significance. Indeed some counties and towns
are so rich in material that each would require
a chapter of their own to cover them
adequately. Whilst excusing my omissions I
should mention one aspect of environmental
study work which I have made no attempt
to feature, an aspect which is so important
as to merit a volume of its own – the study
of nature and the ways in which the natural
environment can provide source material as
rich and varied as any contained in the pages
which follow.

Finally I would like to stress most firmly
that the aim and purpose of this book is
simply to provide teachers with a starting
point for local research, to indicate
direction rather than to provide a once-and-
for-all solution to the reader who wants to
know how to occupy his third-year slow
readers until they pass from him into the quiet
academic pastures of the secondary modern
school down the road.

In conclusion I must state as a teacher
employed by the Inner London Education
Authority, that the Authority is in no way
responsible for the opinions expressed above –
or in the pages which follow.

June 1970   H.P.

Making a start

"We live in a country that is richer than any other in the visible remains of the past but . . . . Most of us are visually illiterate."

Fieldwork in Local History
by W. G. Hoskins, Faber & Faber, 1967.

Over the past thirty years there has been a subtle change in the way in which knowledge is presented to young children. There was a time when the "school outing" was an annual event, smacking of reward for hard work over the year that had passed and having little or no relevance to what had happened in the classroom. Nowadays it is something of an exception if children are not taken by their teachers to museums and art galleries, to stately homes and factories, to castles and to churches.

An outward looking programme of this sort to some extent reflects the changes which have been happening within the schools themselves. Teachers have begun to realise that young children do not compartmentalise learning into tightly bound subject areas; Science and History, English and Geography, Mathematics, Art and Music all overlap. How do we, for example, present Sir Walter Raleigh to a nine-year-old? Was he simply an explorer (Geography), a Tudor Pirate (History), a writer and poet (English) or was he all of these things and more? When we consider the River Thames with eight-year-olds are we really concerned overmuch with watersheds and bridging points, tidal flows and estuaries or in the broad sweep of the river through the countryside to the sea? And if we feel the latter is more in keeping with the needs of the children we will bring in everything which interests them from Hampton Court Palace to the Greenwich Observatory, from barges to bridges.

This movement away from presenting formalised bodies of knowledge still worries some teachers, though I am sure that once they have freed themselves from the shackles of a formal curriculum. they will discover, to their delight and surprise, that the children know more than they did before when bound by books and blackboard outlines.

Of course I am aware that taking children out — to see, to touch, to feel, to experience — presents a whole host of difficulties. The timetable has often to be altered (or dispensed with altogether), colleagues on the staff might have to accommodate a few extra children, there are problems of finding the money for fares and entrance fees, local authority regulations which have to be complied with and perhaps even insurance cover to be arranged. To skate over these things and dismiss them as irrelevant to my thesis would be shortsighted, for I am only too aware that these are the very arguments most often advanced against a detailed study of the neighbourhood and the countryside beyond.

The timetable is the headteacher's concern and how it is implemented will largely reflect the philosophy on which he runs his school. In some schools an integrated day operates with little difficulty because both the building and the teachers within it see school as a place in which artificial barriers (such as those imposed by time or an adult-directed curriculum) are hindrances to children's learning. In others, the old formal regime of my own childdood remains, so much Maths followed by so much English followed by so much History (with Art thrown in as an occasional Friday afternoon makeweight). Between these two extremes lie the majority of our Primary Schools — with large blocks of time set aside for specific activities.

Plate 2
*On one short walk five-year-olds wonder
at a crane . . .*

Plate 3
talk about a market . . .

Plate 4
and meet a horse. All these experiences
provide starting points for creative work.

Plate 5
*Having met the horse they learn how his
shoes are made . . .*

Plate 6
*and touch the Lord Mayor of London's
coach which the horse sometimes helps pull.*

Now my observations would suggest that as soon as a class is launched upon a series of local visits, the timetable, however conceived, tends to be forgotten. It is not that Maths and English are never done (indeed in the school in which I work the teachers seem more conscious of omissions on the Maths side and compensate for it by doing far more than they perhaps need to do), but rather that they fit naturally into the broad study which is under way. Of course, when children have used the market as a starting point and groups of them are producing graphs, editing tape recordings, painting and modelling all in the confines of one room at the same time, it is exceedingly difficult to explain to a doubting headteacher that the Maths period (in which all this is happening) has not been lost forever! Certainly the evidence contained in the Plowden Report echoes the findings of the majority of teachers who have worked in this way – by making the timetable fit the child one achieves far more, far more quickly, than by following a tightly controlled, subject-orientated, teaching programme.

The problems which arise when a teacher goes out with only a part of his class or group can be solved by co-operative or team teaching – and it is well to remember that one does not have to have a purpose-built school to get this under way. If two or more teachers are sharing common areas the possible groupings are as varied as the number of children they are dealing with. Thus if we have 70 children to two teachers we could divide the group 70:0, 69:1, 30:40, 25:45 – and so on. If such a staffing position can be established in a school then one can have groups of children out at almost any time, of any size, without every other teacher in the building being inconvenienced by the "odd bodies that no one wants from Jones' class". The fluid arrangement described above allows for knowledgeable parents to be brought into group work where appropriate. While parents may not have the background of teaching experience necessary to present knowledge

to children in a meaningful way, they often can supply facts so that teacher and children learn together. There are many examples I could give – the engineer in the post office, the zoologist who helped with an animal project, the doctor who gave a fascinating talk at a medical museum on eighteenth-century surgery, the smith (not a local parent but one who belonged to a tiny village school we were visiting in Sussex) who showed London children how to use the forge, make a shoe and finally fix it to the hoof of a long-suffering horse. Again by sharing children between teachers one can keep groups of this sort to a size which does not frighten off those adults in the community who have something to give to children. We are not asking them to do our job, but merely to give information that we may do our job that much better.

I could develop my thesis still further by suggesting that co-operative teaching also allows for the natural assimilation of students and part-time teachers. This again will help reduce the size of groups engaged on any one activity and mean that children are not taken on visits which are irrelevant to them simply because there is no place else for them to go.

The provision of money for fares and entrance fees is a much more difficult problem to solve. One has to remember that education in the state sector is free and that we cannot demand that parents contribute towards the cost of taking children out (though in fact most parents are happy to do so). This means that there must be other avenues for obtaining money. The LEA often includes a small sum in the capitation for this purpose, though it is usually hardly sufficient to take a class on a two-mile bus ride. Then there are school functions from jumble sales to summer draws, Christmas fairs and wool collections. Undoubtedly, although Parent Teacher Associations should not be regarded simply as money-raisers, an active PTA is almost essential if regular sums are to be raised for out of school activities.

Before taking children out I think it imperative that the teacher makes himself familiar with the local authority's regulations. There is tremendous variation between one LEA and another. Some require advance notification of all visits, others lay down detailed requirements on the size of group, the number of accompanying adults, the age of the children etc. To break regulations without knowing what they are is surely foolhardy and could lead to quite unnecessary heartache. If insurance needs to be taken out, the School Journey Association (23, Southampton Way, London W.C.1.) offers a wide range of suitable policies.

Let me now consider how best we can plan a programme of visits for the children with whom we work. I firmly believe that though we should relate the visits to the age of the children concerned, there is no point in taking children out with the sole purpose of filling up gaps in their knowledge of local history, local geography or local culture. One cannot plan for children's reaction to a happening. One group of seven-year-olds will be fired by a visit to a railway marshalling yard, a second group might well find the men digging a deep hole outside the school gate far more worthy of their interest.

Broadly speaking I believe that any environmental study should begin immediately around the school. This is obviously applicable to children of five or six – but how often do we take older children on long journeys to visit another town when they are quite ignorant of the community in which they themselves live ? Indeed when the study is really local the children often have much to offer – from old family photographs and newspaper cuttings to stories handed down from parent and grandparent.

In this connection nine- and ten-year-olds will often find the school log book of interest, and if the school dates back to Victorian times

there will be much worth commenting upon. Even if the school has only been recently opened its name might prompt research.

As knowledge of the immediate locality deepens, the distance which the children are taken from the school can be increased. Local studies – which could include work on such things as churches, markets, street names, and transport services – can be used to show the group how the knowledge acquired can be recorded as well as giving them valuable experience on such things as the use of reference books, maps and local archives.

Whilst on the subject of local study I should like to touch upon a number of topics which I have not considered within the main body of the book. Every town (and many villages) in England boasts a statue or two. Often these commemorate the life of local worthies who have some claim to fame, even if their names are not always included in school history books. These statues often provide fascinating starting points for individual topic work. Who was this man ? When did he live ? What did he do ? What can I find out about him in the library or county museum ? Does anyone in the town remember him ? I do not propose to give a lengthy list but the following examples will serve to illustrate my point:– John Bunyan, the nonconformist writer, and John Howard, the prison reformer (Bedford), Alfred the Great (Wantage), John Hampden of Ship Money fame (Aylesbury), John Trevithick the engineer (Camborne, Cornwall), William Barnes, poet and antiquarian (Dorchester), Edward Wilson, the explorer (Cheltenham), Robert Raikes the founder of Sunday Schools (Gloucester), Isaac Watts, Anglican hymnwriter (Southampton), Charles Gordon, soldier (Chatham), William Harvey, the physician who discovered the circulation of the blood (Folkestone), Thomas Paine, philosopher (Thetford), Thomas Gainsborough, artist (Sudbury, Suffolk).

This particular aspect of environmental study – people – can be further developed by the teacher making himself aware of the writings of local authors. For example, is it possible to teach in Dorchester and not bring Thomas Hardy to the children's notice, or London and not use Pepys and Evelyn ? Written material of this sort can be supplemented from other sources (e.g. Jonathan Cape's "Jackdaw" series; G. Tawney's *Select Documents from English Economic History).*

Then, within the classroom, the teacher should attempt to support local excursions with small collections which are relevant to studies already under way or which he hopes, by their very nature, will provoke enquiry and research. Thus a collection of old transport documents (e.g. photographs of trams, bus tickets, a timetable, a route map, an Edwardian poster) might be displayed to encourage questioning or merely to consolidate knowledge already acquired.

Finally let us assume that we are about to embark on a detailed study of the locality. We have everything in readiness. We have mounted a display or two, the children are eager, the headteacher willing. Is there anything else to think of ? I would suggest that there is – two small points which are often overlooked and yet which can, by their very omission, cause the whole programme to come to an abrupt halt.

It is important, if children are to be expected to work out of doors, that they are given adequate materials to work with. I will develop this in the next chapter, but would make the point here that we should not expect children to take adequate notes or make sketches if they have no boards to rest their papers on or a sharpener for their pencils.

Secondly, it is always advisable to make sure that the place we are to visit is both open and able to receive our party. There's nothing worse than to get to a church and find a funeral in progress or to a museum and find the section we need closed for redecoration !

Plate 7
*Our churches contain many examples of the
work of artists in silver...*

Plate 8
in wood...

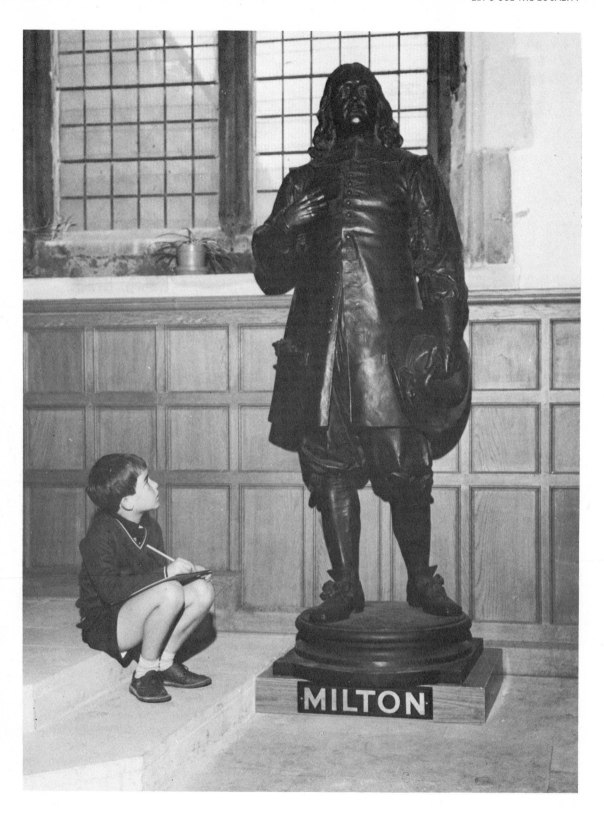

Plate 9
and in stone,

Plate 10
as well as written history . . .

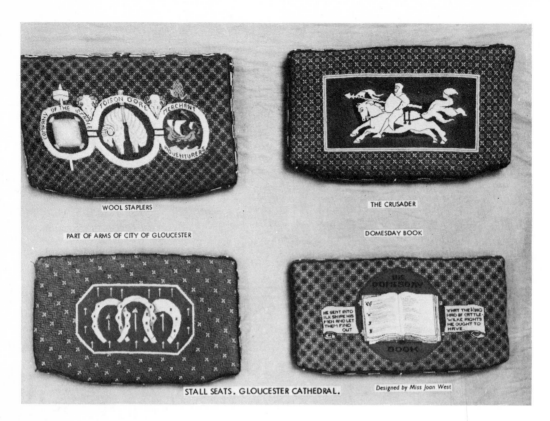

WOOL STAPLERS

THE CRUSADER

PART OF ARMS OF CITY OF GLOUCESTER

DOMESDAY BOOK

STALL SEATS. GLOUCESTER CATHEDRAL.

Designed by Miss Joan West

Plate 11
and history in pictures.

Plate 12
Taking a brass rubbing. Ten-year-olds.
Photo by courtesy 'Art and Craft in Education'.

Plate 13 (overleaf)
Taking a tombstone rubbing. Eight and
nine-year-olds.

Recording the experience

As I see it, there are two quite different times when children will need to be given material to record their experience – when they are actually on site and when they have returned to school. Let me examine each of these in detail, for each will require different equipment and knowledge of different techniques.

When taking children to work out of doors I believe that it is essential to provide them with drawing materials which offer more scope than notebook and pencil. Children find it far easier to work large then to work small provided, that is, that the art climate of the school is such as to encourage the use of paper larger than $11\frac{1}{2}" \times 7"$!

Thus I would recommend that on most visits a range of sugar papers is taken. The size and shape of the sheets should be varied so that children can choose the piece which best fits what they wish to record. Attention should also be paid to the colour of the papers available. Pale blue papers, for example, make it far easier for a child to capture the feel of a seascape than neutral grey, while red paper is ideal for recording the impression of Tudor brickwork, as is deep slate if the aim is to capture the coldness of Caen stone.

To work out of doors on paper as large as $20" \times 30"$ will mean that crayons or oil pastels will also need to be made available. Although I have taken "wet colours" with me on school visits, I feel that they are more bother than they are worth, especially if the group is travelling by public transport. However, as wax crayons (the Finart/Freart range from Cosmic Crayon Co is ideal) are now available in so wide a range of colours, there is really no limit to the fine tones which can be obtained.

Young children will prefer to work in a single colour on pastel paper. Varied effects can be achieved by giving the crayon pictures a colour wash* on return to school.

Crayons are also invaluable because they can be used for texture rubbings. For this, detail paper will be required. The surface from which a rubbing is to be taken is first dusted with a soft cloth. Place the detail paper over the brass, stone or plaque and hold in place either with strips of Sellotape or lead weights – though on some vertical surfaces additional hands are the best method (Plate 13). The paper should be taut and pucker-free. Feel the edge of the design and rub the crayon in firm even strokes over the paper covering the actual design, all the strokes being made in the same direction. When the rubbing has been completed, carefully remove the paper. This technique may be used to obtain texture rubbings of tombstones, brasses, wall plaques, commemorative plates, decorative brickwork and ironwork – in fact anything which has texture.

Rubbings may also be taken on detail paper with white crayon. To make the design reappear is quite simple. On return to school pin the rubbing onto a flat surface and brush Ebony Stain or black fountain pen ink (*not* Indian ink) over the whole paper. The white waxed areas will resist the stain, making the design appear against a black surround. When the stain has dried, cut round the rubbing and paste onto a mounting board.

One word of caution. It is necessary to obtain permission before rubbings are taken of church brasses, for indiscriminate rubbing can do irreparable damage.

*Technically this is a wax resist.

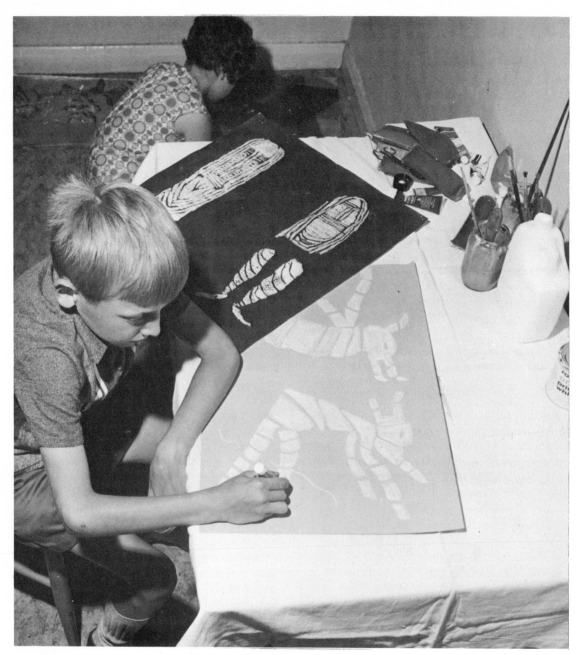

Plate 14
Rubbings and textures can be taken in white
crayon and resisted in Ebony stain. Ralph,
aged eight, was inspired by some carvings
on the base of a Saxon cross.

Drawings and rubbings can be supplemented by oral and written work. Sometimes I simply suggest that children use a portable tape recorder to speak their impressions, to note facts from museum notices, to tape the talk given by the expert or to interview people who work on the site. Yet, if the situation warrants it, I also think that there is a place for written work. Standing in the dungeon of a castle, or looking down from an allure walk, sitting in front of a portrait of Elizabeth I or being overwhelmed by the noise of the generators in a power station — are the sort of situations I have in mind. The writings might simply be a collection of words which evoke what the child is feeling, a prose description or a piece of verse — in any event they will be lively first impressions which will be invaluable for further work on return to school.

Another useful, though rarely used, piece of equipment is the camera. Children often show surprising skill in handling 35 mm models, particularly if a fairly foolproof lightmeter is incorporated*. Colour slides, particularly if taken by the children themselves, certainly aid recall as well as adding a new dimension to the work. If black and white prints are taken from the transparencies one also has another source of display material.

While on any visit it is important for the teacher to look for things which could be useful for follow-up work in school. Post cards, slides, guidebooks, photographs, plans and maps are perhaps too obvious to need mentioning. But these "bought" things could well be supplemented with an equally valuable collection of things found — corks from fishermen's nets, an interesting stone, some pottery sherds, the basket-maker's reeds, a fossil, a nail from the smith, a withy from a fence maker. Whenever one takes children to the country, there will be flowers to collect, leaves and bark to rub, and all manner of nature specimens to uncover. Though this is essentially a book about the way man has worked upon and changed the natural

*Halina and Kodak both make reasonably priced models.

environment, not to let children find flowers because one is at an old castle or an eighteenth-century windmill is surely shortsighted.

All of this brings me to perhaps the one area in which we feel most uncertain. To what extent should we direct the children's eyes to this or that exhibit in a museum, this or that feature of a castle ? To say "Look at this and draw it" is as narrowing as the Dotheboys Hall approach of "Winders, clean 'em". Do children need to record the same things in the same way so that we can say "This they have learned" ? I know that there are some children who would perhaps never appear to have done anything if there was no "list of exhibits to find and make notes on". But perhaps we need to discover for these children another way of looking, giving them another vehicle (or technique) through which to express themselves.

I have heard it suggested — by much more erudite educationalists than myself — that the value of any visit, any happening, lies in the impact it has upon the child, an impact which is within him, which cannot be measured or marked, or painted or written about. This for me is rather too romantic — but I appreciate the point. As an adult I can wonder at the skill of a Norman stonemason, gaze with awe at a Leonardo cartoon, be transported by a Mozart symphony — but please don't ask me to draw my experiences !

On return to school the visit should be discussed in detail before any follow-up work is attempted. Children have a tremendous need to verbalise — yet too often the first thing they have to do is "write it up".

The discussion could begin by encouraging each child to talk about the things they saw, smelt, touched, heard, tasted (the last sense being included only if relevant !) This could lead to an awareness of what they wanted to communicate about the experience. Is it best to use words, to make a model or to paint a picture ? For each child there will be a different way, a way uniquely his own, a way which allows for emotion to show through the work. This means, of course, that the classroom should contain a wide range of materials so that children are not frustrated by being unable to find the very things they need to communicate how they really feel.

Let me illustrate this point. I took some children to the Stour valley and we spent some time in the village of Dedham. Some of the group went to the Flemish Weavers' House and drew and measured, took rubbings and wrote descriptions of the woodwork, the courtyard and the old pump. Another group had chosen the church as the starting point for discovery, while others were concentrating upon the old buildings in the High Street, making maps and taking measurements. Two other groups had decided upon quite different approaches to the area. Armed with a tape recorder, they asked local inhabitants about John Constable, about changes they had seen in the village in their lifetime. The second group, who had looked at the River at Flatford, went down to the mill at Dedham.

Now it is quite obvious that a "write about yesterday's visit" approach would not have served any real purpose. The children who had spent the best part of three hours at the Weavers' cottage had a mass of information to present – through models, scale plans, historical notes and in drawings of the house from a variety of viewpoints. The "church group" wanted to compile a guide. How could this best be done – individually, in pairs, or would each child deal with a particular aspect of the building for incorporation into a group folder ? The map-makers' task was quite clear – to present an accurate map showing the village in detail. What scale would best suit their purpose ? Could it be a "picture map" ? And then there was the river group – were their experiences in any way similar to the others ? They had seen things certainly – baby ducks, rippling water, fish rising. But one can't model

these things or draw them. Such experiences might well end by being recorded in sound through the children's own music making – their music supporting or adding a new dimension to the poetry and prose which has flowed from the experience of being a city child submerged by country sounds. Here are a few examples.

ON THE STOUR THEN AND NOW

Then the trees made way for horses,
Pulling barges to and fro.
Nowadays the trees are growing
Branches overhanging low.

Then were barges on the river
Then were barges on the Stour
Now the waters calm and peaceful
Now the barges are no more.

Then Constable painting the river
Then a horse pulling a barge
Now the bridge is very much wider
Now no horses but coaches large.
(Nine-year-old)

THE SUN

We were looking at the water
The ducks were wet and hungry
Ducking their heads down
In search of food
The rain was still coming down
Suddenly the water rippled
A silver disc was reflected in the water
Surrounded by blue
A break in the grey clouds
It was the sun
The rain had stopped
The sun had come out.
(Eight-year-old)

LOOKING AT A PICTURE (by Constable)

I sit in the boat while the boy struggles to paddle it along. It is a dull day and the trees overhead look like giants, big and black. There are three cows walking towards my home, the cottage. I am nearly there now and see my three sisters and the dog playing on the lawn.
(Ten-year-old)

THE SKY AT DEDHAM

Clouds, dull black trying to spread themselves across the sky, White grey ones, running away from the black. A storm is coming. It's evening. The clouds are dark and dull.
(Seven-year-old)

FLATFORD – MAY 1970

We arrived at Flatford, Suffolk. It was trying to rain. The ducks wet and bedraggled, searching for food. We stood on the bridge looking out on the water. Suddenly the water ripples and a beam of light reflects on the water. The sun is out at last.
(Eight-year-old)

Work of this type places a bigger burden on the teacher than if he were content to work in a less diffuse way. In addition to providing a variety of picture and model-making materials, he must also create a climate in which individual children feel secure enough to express themselves in prose and verse, paint and pastel – the very areas in which a child is most sensitive to criticism or to thoughtless comment.

When children have completed their study of a particular place how should it be presented? Too often, it seems to me, we are a little wayward in our treatment of children's painting and written work. The display should aim at communicating something of the group's experience. "We went to Fountains Abbey. This is what we have learned".

We can enhance the appearance of the children's work by careful selection of their pictures, models, poetry and prose. I don't think we need to "stick everything up", though it is important that something from everybody is included. The selection need not be the teacher's. Children can be just as ruthless in their rejection of material. The following simple hints, however, might prove useful whoever makes the final choice.

(a) Cover the display board with backing paper or fabric which will blend with the topic being featured, e.g. deep olive green will give an attractive backing for rubbings worked in gold crayon, blue for seascapes, brown for architectural pen and ink studies. All types of paper are suitable for covering display boards – though wallpaper is perhaps the most effective.

(b) Trim and mount the pictures before display.

(c) Marry children's work with material from other sources, e.g. an adult artist's impression of a village displayed near a child's drawing. This means that such things as photographs, post cards and newspaper cuttings should be seen as valuable additions to the children's recorded experiences.

(d) Use a staple tacker or pin pusher to mount the work. Four large brass drawing pins in the corners of a 2" × 2" pen and ink sketch hardly help us see it as a thing of beauty.

(e) Display notices should be uniform throughout. Felt pens are so much easier to handle than the more traditional lettering media, although they do not give the delicate flow of line obtainable with a lettering pen.

(f) Include books in the display. These could be books made by the children or reference books which have been used in the study – and how much better a book table looks when given a table cloth and perhaps a bowl of flowers (Plate 25).

It has been said that the aim of the Primary School Teacher should be to make "the classroom a child's place, a workshop, a place which is his own".

How better can we achieve this ideal than by using the children's experiences for creative work of all kinds which within the classroom environment are extended, deepened and vivified ?

Plate 15
Visiting a 14th-century pub . . .
Photo by courtesy Studio John Norman, King's Lynn

Plate 16
and meeting 20th-century pigs.
Photo by courtesy Studio John Norman,
King's Lynn.

Plate 17
A metre square plot...

Plate 18
will reveal a wealth of interesting material

Plate 19
and lead us into the mathematics of sampling

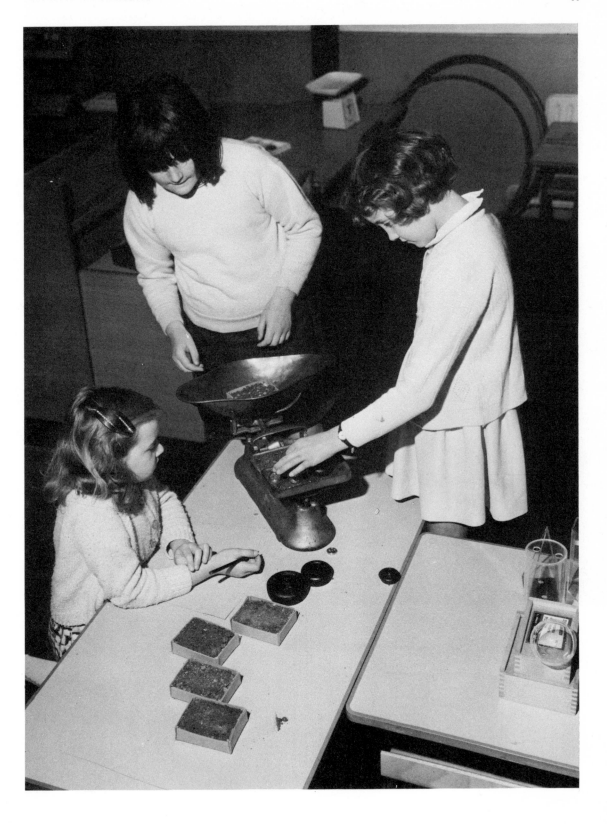

Plate 20
and map-making. Eight-, nine- and ten-year-olds.

Plate 21
Taking a traffic count. Nine-year-olds.

Plate 22 (overleaf)
The pulpit at St Stephens Walbrook,
20 by 30 in. Deborah, aged eight, liked to
work in pencil and crayon.

Plate 23 (overleaf)
Cranes 12 by 10 in. Keith, aged six, preferred
cutting into thick crayon.

Plate 24
*Visiting the police horses 30 by 12 in. by
Sandra, aged seven, in oil pastel and paint.*

Plate 25
*Hampton Court Palace 50 by 30 in.
Group work (seven- and eight-year-olds) in
acrylic paint and tissue.*

Plate 26
'We visited some Georgian houses' 85 by 60 in.
Group work (nine-year-olds) paper collage.

Plate 27
The Tower of London 60 by 60 in.
Group work (five- to nine-year-olds). The
younger children supplied the picture, the
older ones the writing.

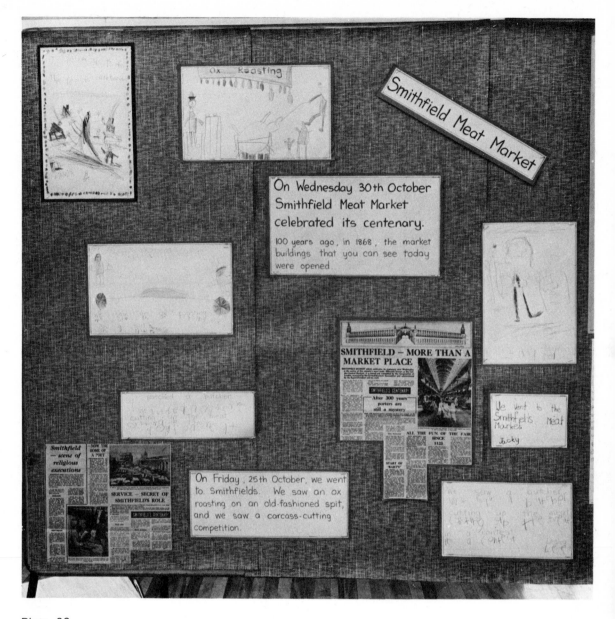

Plate 28
Recording the experience 1. Five-year-olds.
Notice that the display unites children's
writing, teachers' titles and newspaper extracts.

Plate 29
Recording the experience 2
Seven- and eight-year-olds.

Plate 30
Recording the experience 3
Six, seven, eight- and nine-year-olds.

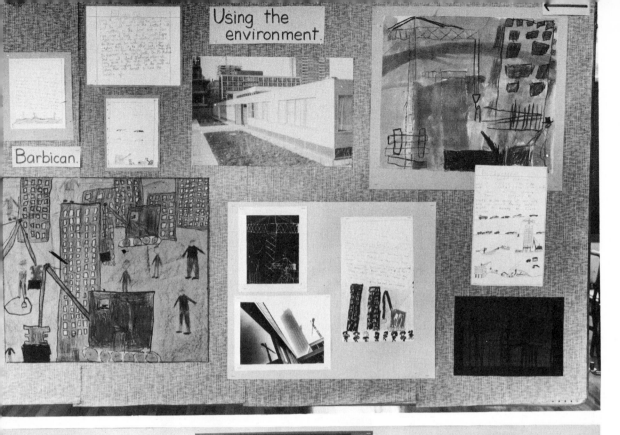

Using the
environment.

Barbican.

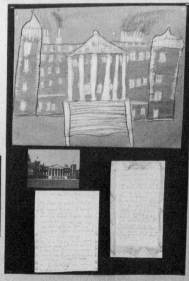

Osterley
Park
House

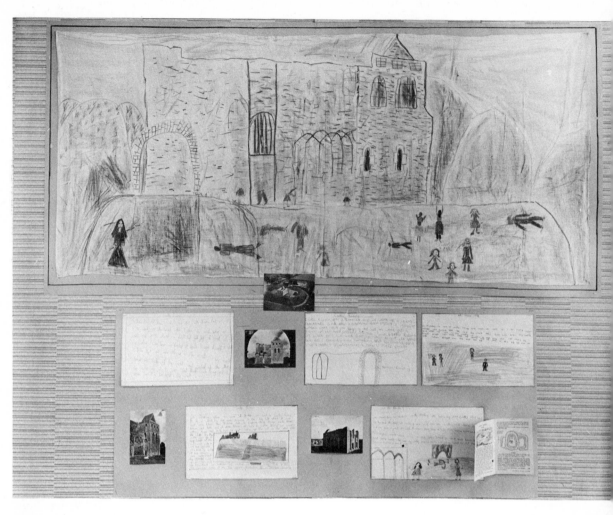

Plate 31
Recording the experience 4
A visit to Norfolk recorded in fabric, in words
and in sketch, with postcards and leaflets.
Eight-, nine- and ten-year-olds.

Plate 32
Recording the experience 5
A visit to a bird sanctuary. Here felt pens
were used for many of the drawings.
Ten- and eleven-year-olds.

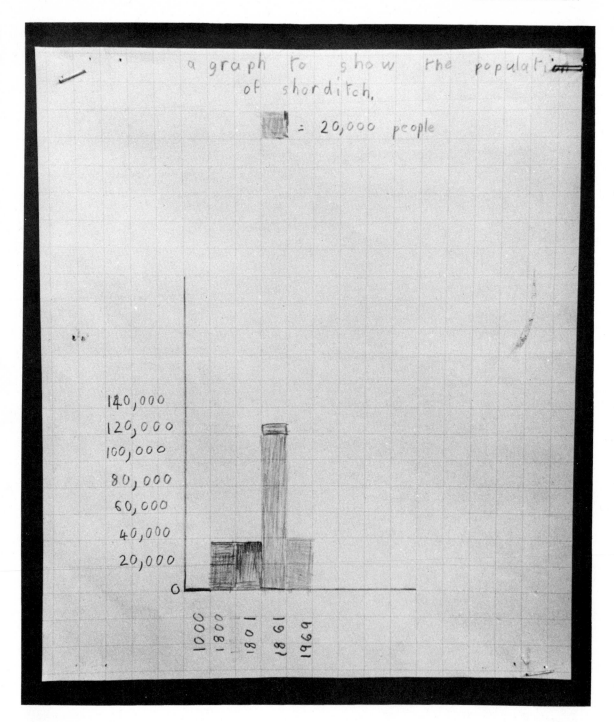

Plate 33
Recording information obtained from local population statistics. Eight-year-old.

Plate 34
Recording information on tape following a visit to the blacksmith (see Plates 5). Five-year-olds.

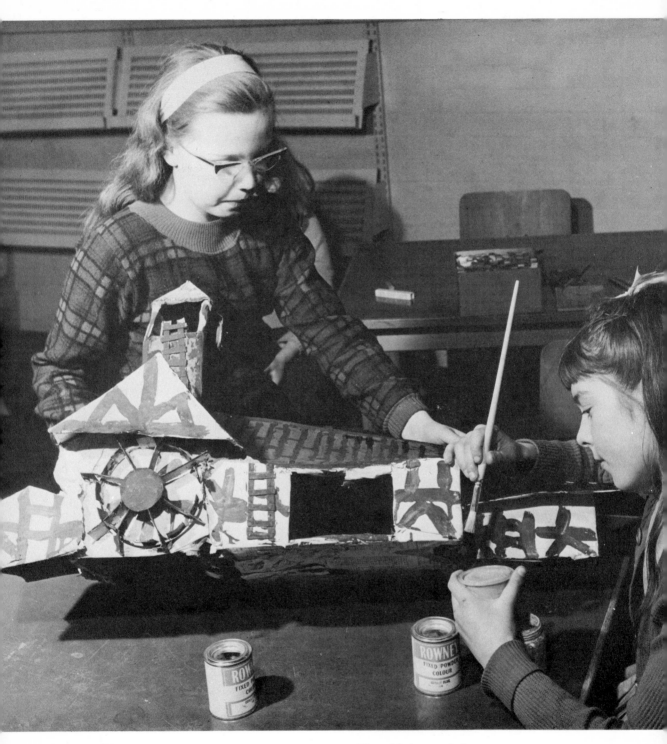

Plate 35
Model-making — a mill. Nine-year-olds.

Plate 36 (opposite)
Model-making — a lock.
Eight- and nine-year-olds.

Plate 37
*Model-making – Georgian furniture. Some
children enjoy working on a small scale.
The fourposter beds were only 10 in high.
Eight- and nine-year-olds.*

Plate 38
*Interesting things can be brought into the
classroom, seven- to ten-year-olds,*

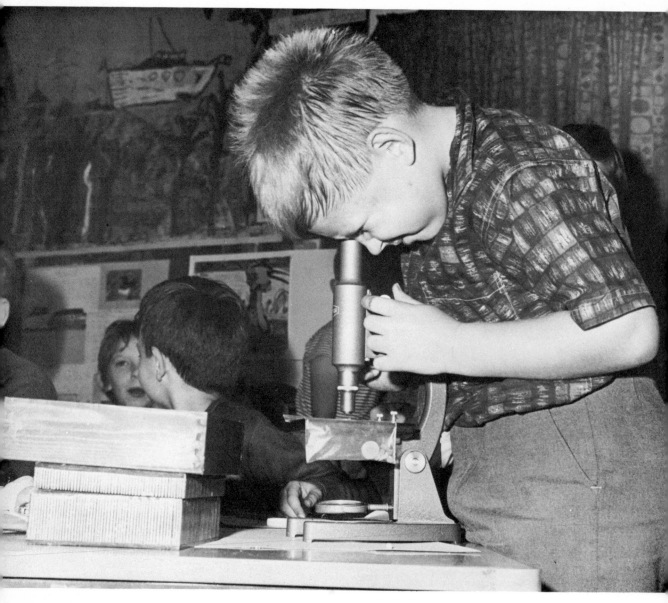

Plate 39
*and though a microscope adds a new
dimension to looking, seven-year-old,*

Plate 40
*it can never capture the wonders of a roof
such as this at Berkeley Castle.*

*Shape, pattern, hue
Age on to age unto these
Keeping steadfastly true*
                                    W. de la Mare

*Photo by G. D. Freke, reproduced by kind
permission of Major R. J. G. Berkeley.*

AUTHOR'S NOTE

Units 1, 2 and 3 are in the most part complementary. Whether we live in a city, town or village we require certain identical services (e.g. the provision of a water supply, transport, law and order), rely on shops and market places as an easy means of obtaining the basic necessities of life and find it convenient to name our streets and number our houses. City, town and village have schools and churches, banks and burial grounds, pubs and vicarages, and it would be pointless to include similar ideas under each heading. Therefore, I have deliberately omitted some obvious areas of study from one unit because it is adequately covered elsewhere. Thus suggestions for the study of the local community around the school are included in the village section although the suggestions are equally pertinent to the teacher who works in the centre of an industrial conurbation. What is Islington or Hampstead but a village submerged by London, or Edgbaston but a village lost in Birmingham ?

Essentially then, units 1 to 3 should be regarded as a single section, and the thoughtful teacher will read all three before embarking on a neighbourhood study.

UNIT 1

The village

Even if the school is situated in the middle of a great industrial complex, the majority of the children will be aware that not everybody chooses (or needs!) to live in towns. The country is never beyond reach and even on a day trip the study of a village will more than repay the time and effort expended.

How we begin our study really depends upon how familiar the children are with the area. If the school is in the village then there will be much common knowledge to be pooled, shared and sifted. If the children are new to the locality (e.g. on a school journey) the starting point may well stem from some specific interest (e.g. geographical siting, the name of the village, or its topographical peculiarities).

Let us examine some of the possible avenues of approach, bearing in mind that my headings could be used as study topics for group work rather than as complete projects for class activities.

(1) The site of the village

This is a difficult aspect for children to study unaided. County histories will provide much source material though it is often in a rather indigestible form. It is useful to remember that, broadly speaking early British settlements were situated on the tops of hills, while the later Saxon villages tended to hug the lower slopes of the valleys. On marshy ground (e.g. the Fens) villages were built on dry "islands" (only visible nowadays when the land is extensively flooded as in the East Coast Floods of 1952). Some villages grew up along rivers,

which made transport easier, others along ancient highway routes, others around a castle (e.g. Corfe, Dorset) or around a local industry like mining (Worth, Dorset), or fishing.

A current Ordnance Survey map will be of value here. Is the village a tight little community with a few houses, a shop and the school close to the church and the village green ?*

This pattern, which we tend to think of as a typical English village, is common in communities which were predominantly agricultural. In areas which were once heavily wooded, houses were built in clearings and villages of this type which spread along a valley may be described as "scattered". Has the village we are studying anything in common with the examples I have given or, better still, in other villages nearby ?

Comparisons of early maps (e.g. local estate maps, maps by Speed, Pont and their successors) with their modern counterparts will show something of the changing patterns of settlement and land utilisation indicating such things as the development of roads and railways, the decay of a mining community, the enclosure of a common or the growth of an estate. Early local maps are often available from the County Archivist, and Xerox copies are usually obtainable at very low cost. The Ordnance Survey maps of Prehistoric, Iron Age,

---

Some authorities suggest that the village green has its roots in pre-Saxon times when it was necessary to safeguard the animals at night by driving them on to a central patch of grass which was surrounded by houses.

Roman, Dark Age, Monastic and Mediaeval Britain will also prove useful. Although their scale is too small for detailed local study, they do indicate something of our slow evolution as a nation – and the development or decay of the village, town or city is part of that evolutionary process.

(2) Land utilisation

The only complicated thing about this aspect of the study is its title. What are the village buildings used for ? How many shops, houses, workshops ? Is there a garage, a cinema, a church, a chapel, a hall ? Are the farms mainly arable or is there visible evidence of sheep, cows, pigs or poultry ? Obviously if the school is in the village all sorts of interesting maths work can flow from a study of this kind, extended perhaps to a survey of where the children's parents work – within the village community or outside it.

(3) Local occupations and crafts

Villages do not contain as many local craftsmen as they once did, but there are often untapped riches in a village community which are rarely realised to the full. Although local farms and dairies would come high on my list, I am also thinking here of all those local craftsmen who have much to pass on to children . . . The ditcher and hedger, for example, often has a fund of knowledge about local birds and small mammals. The certain movements of the basket-makers' hands are a revelation in themselves. Again I would emphasise that it is important to meet these people on their own ground rather than drag them into school to talk (which they have not been trained to do). A portable tape recorder is a very valuable piece of equipment for visits of this type.

Villages on the coast or those which are closely associated with particular industries (e.g. Honiton – weaving: Worth – quarrying) will

have areas for study uniquely their own. Fishermen, their boats, nets, lobster and crab pots are invariably popular; mining villages often have a rich verbal heritage (interviewing the oldest miner about his childhood or stories told him by his father or grandfather is an invaluable way of learning how the community has developed).

Geddington Cross, Northamptonshire

(4) **Buildings of interest**

The church and the inn are considered individually (Units 5 and 7). However, most villages have at least one of the following meriting further study:

(a) Preaching, market or commemorative cross – which may be Saxon (as at Sandbach, Cheshire), mediaeval (Eleanor Cross, Geddington, Northants) or comparatively modern (The Banbury Cross, Banbury, Oxfordshire).

(b) Signposts, milestones, bench marks. The more eccentric place names are often a source of amusement and research.

(c) Village lock-ups. These are to be found in all shapes and sizes. Their original purpose has often been forgotten, though many now bear a plaque commemorating the fact (e.g. as at Swanage, Dorset).

(d) Almshouses, local charities (too common to list in detail).

(e) Village signs, county signs. Norfolk is perhaps *the* county for village signs, particularly around the Royal Estate at Sandringham. Village signs often tell something of the history and occupation of the people of the neighbourhood and should never be ignored.

(f) Historic trees. To my mind the one with the greatest claim to fame is the one at Tolpuddle, Dorset, which has links with the growth of Trade Unionism in England. On a more romantic note Charles II seems to have spent an incredible amount of time hiding in oak trees in various parts of the country.

Village pump

(g) Village well, village pump. Here we have the opportunity to compare our modern water supply with that enjoyed by our ancestors, at the same time introducing the idea of links between impure water and disease.

(h) Village pound – once used for stray cattle.

(i) Tithe barns. These are now, more often than not, part of a local farm (e.g. Binham, Norfolk). However, fine examples can still be seen at Glastonbury, Somerset, Abbotsbury, Dorset, and Great Coxwell, Berkshire.

Tithe Barn (Bradford-on-Avon, Wiltshire)

(5) The use of common materials

If we travel across a county like Glamorgan or through the Cotswolds we note that each village has a similar character – a character imposed upon it by the materials which have been used in its construction. Before the coming of the railways the majority of buildings in any community were of necessity built from local material (local stone, for example, being readily available and the skill to use it almost inbred). The children will find it worthwhile to study the materials used in local buildings, for they too contain clues to man's past. Why do we find granite being used in Devon, limestone in the Cotswolds, timber and bricks in Warwickshire, flint in Norfolk, lath and clay in parts of Suffolk, timber lap facing in Essex ? Why is stone slab used for roofing in some areas while tile, slate or straw is preferred in others ? Why are dry stone walls common to the Yorkshire Dales, so rare in Surrey and Middlesex ?

(6) Roads, footpaths and bridleways

A simple plan of the village is essential for any study. A large rough could be prepared by the teacher for discussion and a quantity of small maps duplicated for individual use. A local study may throw up interesting street names (see Unit 3) but its value lies in the fact that it makes children aware of the general topography of the area.

Large scale maps may be made to include children's drawings of the village.

First prepare a large scale street map on a display board. (The bigger the map the easier will it be to complete with accuracy.) Paint in the streets, fields, gardens etc., in pale washes of colour. Individual children are then given the task of sketching accurately all the buildings and monuments which fall within the map's limit. On returning to school these are redrawn on cartridge paper, coloured and cut out. Finally the paper cut-outs are pasted onto the street plan – walls, gates, farm machines and even people being added to make the picture "come to life" (See diagram opposite).

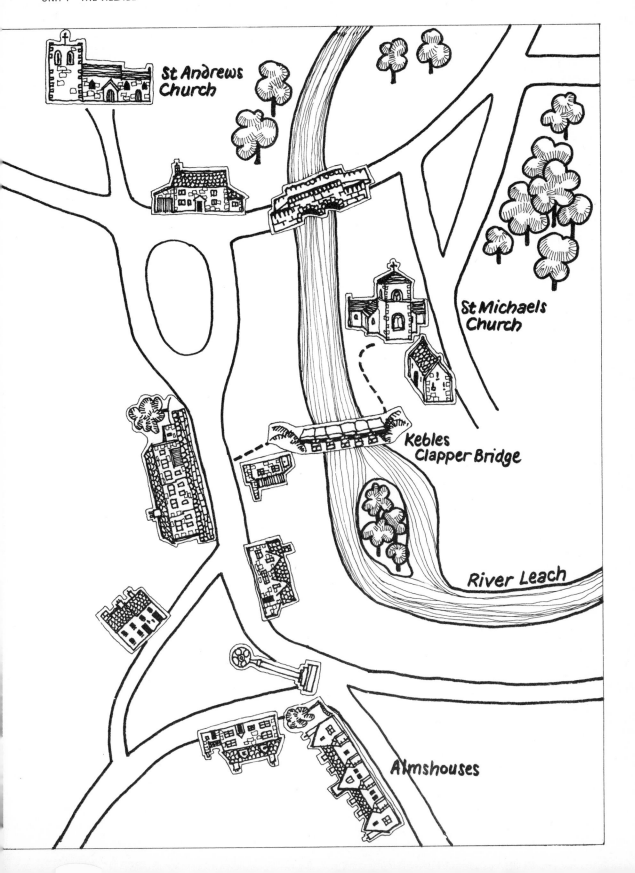

UNIT 2

The town today

When studying a village, children are helped by the fact that most small communities have a character of their own. I suppose that this is because the site itself is usually tightly defined which makes it possible to relate (without undue difficulty) such things as street with street, shop with church, bank with hall. Towns by comparison tend to be rather anonymous places.

However, if we begin with this rather disturbing viewpoint, there is nothing much we will be able to do to make the locality come alive for the children we teach — whether we work in post-war Stevenage or Edwardian Northampton.

I would begin by trying to capture something of the atmosphere of the area immediately around the school (which is, in essence, the community from which the school draws its pupils). Explore the streets around the school, making a map to illustrate the position of houses, shops, churches and factories (see Page 65). Photographs could also be taken to support the study. This might well result in children being able to identify themselves with particular parts of the map . . . "this is John's house", "our street" (set material here for the Maths lesson) "the factory in which six of our fathers work", "Mary's uncle's garage".

Children could also try to find out when the house they live in was built. There might be a plaque on the wall somewhere (Albert Villas 1851) or a document or a map on the development in the local library . . . in prosperous areas a house deed might be available for inspection. Churches and chapels were often built at the same time as the estates and this in turn might provide a valid reason for visiting the remnants of ecclesiastical Victoriana which still dominate the suburbs of our larger towns. The church records themselves will contain much local history, even if they only serve to indicate periods of hardship (e.g. cholera in the 1850s) or expectancy of life in earlier decades.

The very localised approach is valuable even if the town in which the school is situated is steeped in history, for it gives the children some idea of how to attempt a study of a larger area. For example, if working with children of secondary age it would be possible to divide the town into sections (perhaps following the parish boundaries) each section being the responsibility of a particular group.

We can also look at the town through the people who live in it. Although families have become more mobile since the second world war, grandparents still enjoy a prominent place in the lives of young children. If the family has lived in the area for many years, grandparents can contribute much of value to the study, portable tape recorders being used to record impressions of town life fifty or sixty years ago. If supporting photographs can be borrowed, so much the better! (I find old people have an almost inexhaustible supply.) The photographs themselves may be used as source materials for children's pictures (dress, transport, housing) or carefully mounted to support their own written work.

These oral sources should never be despised, particularly as old people often remember their own childhood quite clearly . . . . and, of course, if they remember stories told them about the neighbourhood by *their* grandparents* we may have managed to span 130 years or more.

Whilst on this aspect of the study it is worth remembering that local people can also give the children some understanding of services which they perform for the community – in such fields as electricity, gas and water supply, law and order and communication. On the whole public services are prepared to co-operate very closely with schools. For example, I have taken five- and six-year-olds to a police stable, seven-year-olds to a fire station, eight-year-olds to a river police H.Q., nine-year-olds to the Post Office Tower, ten-year-olds to an electricity generating station. In each case the numbers were kept as small as possible, several visits being made so that as many children as possible could benefit from the experience.

The knowledge gained from these visits was recorded on returning to school. The younger children preferred to paint pictures of their experiences, but even at this stage it was supported by a considerable amount of written work (Plates 27, 28). Older children should, of course, be encouraged to take a small notebook in which to record on the spot observations – and how much easier it is for them to make notes if they are also given a piece of hardboard to rest on!

It is worth remembering that not all work places are suitable for parties of young children to visit. Local education authorities as well as public service departments usually follow a code of regulations, designed to protect teacher and taught. For example, one can't take a nine-year-old down a coalmine, or over a gas works or on the G.P.O. underground railway. On the other hand you might be lucky enough to persuade the local police to demonstrate traffic control and road safety in your school playground with car, motor cycles and traffic lights.

Although not all public services are able to provide facilities for school parties, most of them are generous in their supply of visual aids, film strips, loops, charts, booklets and films. Often speakers will be prepared to come to school to talk about their work, and although this is not as good as a visit it at least provides a tangible link with the real world.

NOTES ON PLACE NAMES

The fact that it is possible to buy a Concise Oxford Dictionary of place names indicates perhaps something of the dangers of attempting to provide a short guide like the one which follows. However, having said that, I have found that children are interested in facts like those which follow-–

Borough, burgh, bury	A fortified camp, a fortified house or town
Beck	Road (Norwegian)
Bourne	A small river (e.g. Winterbourne, the place where a river runs only in winter)

*In 1969 I chanced to meet Sir Harry Verney in the chapel at Claydon House. He spoke of his boyhood, of Florence Nightingale and the stories she told of the Crimean War. Florence spent much time in the house . . . an outstanding example of oral history.

Breck	Hill	Lake	Water, usually fed by a stream
Bridge	A crossing place	Lan, llan	A place associated with a saint (used as a prefix)
By	Village		
Chester, caster, cester	A fortified place		
Combe	Valley	Leigh, ley lay	An open space
Cott, cot, cotte	Cottage or place of shelter	Port	A market place
		Scale	A hut
Dale	Valley	Slack	A valley
Den	A valley or a place where animals were grazed	Spital	A hospital, a place for lepers
		Stock, stoke	A place
Don	A hill	Stow	A holy place e.g. Felixstowe, the holy place of St. Felix
Fell	A hill		
Field	Open place (e.g. Sheffield, a place for pasturing sheep)	Street	A road, a paved way. This may be used as a prefix (streat, strat) e.g. Stratford, Streeton
Ford	A crossing place		
Gill	A valley	Tarn	Small lake
		Thorpe	Hamlet
Ham	A meadow, a home place, a village	Thwaite	Clearing
Hay	An enclosure in a forest clearing	Toft	Homestead
		Ton, tun	Farm or manor
Head	Implies (sometimes) ancient religious link e.g. Gateshead, a ritual associated with a goat	Tre	A farm (usually prefix)
		Well	a place with a spring
		Wick (inland)	Buildings, often a farm with cows
Ing, ingham	The followers of (e.g. Reading, the place of the followers of Reada; Walsingham, home of the followers of Waels)	Wick (coastal)	A bay
		Worthy	An enclosure round a house

In addition to this basic list, some children
might care to look for evidence of Norman-
French on their local map (Beaumaris,
Rievaulx, Dieulacres) or places with religious
(Abbotsbury, Cerne Abbas) royal (regis) or
military associations (e.g. Temple Combe –
the Knights Templars).

UNIT 3

Towns — history in stone

It would be difficult to use the town as a starting point for a detailed environmental study without delving deeply into local history. The older the child the more detailed the research can be, but even quite young children enjoy hearing stories associated with the area in which they live.

However, in this unit I intend to keep my observations entirely historical, which means that teachers of the very young may find it of limited value.

The history of the town will tend to be closely identified with the reasons behind its growth — be they economic, political or strategic (or a combination of all three). Thus we might ask the following questions:–

Did the town grow up round a fortress ? (Berwick-on-Tweed, Chester, Caernarvon, Carlisle).

Did it grow up to serve the needs of a particular industry ? (Pottery, mining, iron, steel, wool, cotton, coal).

Did it grow up at the crossroads of a trade route ? (Banbury).

Did it grow up as a result of new methods of communication ? (Crewe – railways).

Did it grow up or expand as a centre of Government ? (Ludlow was the seat of the Council of the Marches of Wales; York, of the Council of the North).

Did it grow up at a river crossing ? (Bristol).

If the town is a port did it develop because of a specific trade (e.g. Manchester – cotton; Southampton – wool; Bristol – slaves) or because of some other factor (e.g. Chatham and Plymouth – naval dockyards) ?

Did it grow around a monastery or ecclesiastical centre ? (e.g. St. Albans).

Did it grow around a spa ? (e.g. Bath, Brighton, Tonbridge Wells).

Some of our towns, of course, may be traced to pre-Roman Celtic settlements and in this event we are rather left struggling in the mist of antiquity. Place names, however, provide useful clues (see Page 67). Royal charters are another valuable pointer to a town's development and also serve to indicate how the status of a community has changed over the years. Northleach (Gloucestershire) for example, was granted a charter in 1227 some 80 years before Newcastle-upon-Tyne. Today few people would be able to pinpoint Northleach on a map, whereas Newcastle has an international reputation (if only for the quality of its football team!)

All of the evidence collected as a result of enquiries of the type suggested above will indicate when the first people began to live in the area and how slowly (or quickly) the town grew. Population statistics (the first accurate figures date from 1801) and local maps will also help define its probable limits during any given period.

The streets themselves might well provide evidence of historical development . . . . the direction they run in, even their names. Fleet Street, in London, for example, reminds us of the river which was for years "the city sewer" – while the "Brook Streets" of many a small town follow the curves of long dried up springs.

An alphabetical collection of local street names may provide much material for research, particularly if the town has existed for several centuries. The names might relate to commerce, to industry, to the geographic limits of the old city, to its famous citizens or its church or baronial property.

For example:–

Beau Street, Westgate Street (Bath). Palace Street, Castle Street, Military Road (Canterbury). Botchergate (Carlisle). Northgate, Watergate, Foregate, White Friars (Chester). Milk Street (Exeter). Beauchamp Hill (Leamington). Horsefair Street, Haymarket, Highcross (Leicester). Sheep Street, Mercers Row (Northampton). Castle Meadow, Tombland, Maddermarket (Norwich). Woolpack Lane (Nottingham). St. Aldates, Cornmarket (Oxford). Mayflower Street,

Sidney Street (Plymouth). Holywell Hill, Verulam Road (St. Albans). Abbey Foregate, Murivance Town Walls (Shrewsbury). Cutler Street, Poultry, Jewry Street, Pepys Street, Stone Cutter Street, Sea Coal Lane (City of London).

Collating and displaying the information can be most rewarding. On a large scale local map mount children's drawings of some of the more interesting buildings, together with any relevant rubbings (wall plaques, street name plates, coal and man hole covers), photographs, engravings and written work. Older children (Secondary Schools) would find it profitable to refer to the "Historic Towns Atlas" published in 1970 by Lovell Jones, which traces town development from mediaeval times.

Some thought will also need to be given to how the buildings within the town may best be studied. Obviously they provide much material for drawing and for model-making. But it would be shortsighted to suggest that the whole group follows the same approach. By encouraging children to concentrate upon specific areas of study both the individual and the group benefit. We could, for example, take children to draw a Nash Terrace and return to school with 30 almost identical pictures. How much richer the work would be if some of the children concentrated upon doorways, while others worked on windows, carved motifs or decorated ironwork.

If this is applied to a wider-based town survey, individual studies could be made of such things as chimney pots, doors, windows, shop fronts, street lights, commemorative plaques, statues, post boxes, old advertisements (some buildings in industrial backstreets still proclaim the wonders of long forgotten tonics and elixirs) while others might make detailed notes on changing architectural styles (Plate 1).

In addition to historical plaques, two other pieces of evidence are worth noting. Fire insurance marks (made from tin, brass or lead) began to be mounted on houses after the Great Fire of London of 1666. The marks enabled the Fire Brigades (which were employed by the Insurance Companies) to identify the property for which they were responsible. The effect of the window tax

Georgian window

Georgian doorway

Fire insurance marks

(first introduced in 1697) is also still much in evidence. This tax existed until 1851 and was imposed upon the owners of houses which had more than 6 windows and a rental value of £5 or more .... An odd piece of information which at the very least enables us to date buildings pre or post the Great Exhibition!

Buildings used by the community in general usually merit more detailed study. There might, for example, be a Market Hall (Wymondham, Norfolk), a Guildhall (York), a Custom House (Exeter, Devon), almshouses, a School, (St. Albans, Winchester, Eton) a row of shops (The Rows at Chester, The Pantiles at Tunbridge Wells), a theatre (St. Albans), a cockpit (Denbigh) or a place for taking the waters (Bath).

Industrial areas may be treated in the same way. Factories and railway stations, gas works and lock gates all reflect something of the age in which they were built. All building is in its time contemporary. Back to back houses in narrow airless streets indicate social conscience (the solution of a housing problem) just as much as do our modern "tower blocks in landscaped setting".

The market place (if there be one) is another rich area for study. Although market squares (as at Norwich) are particularly attractive, the central theme has obvious links with the great fairs of mediaeval times. Originally, of course, particular trades mounted their sheds and stalls in tightly defined areas of the town, their temporary 'shops' being put up and

The Rows at Chester

**The Custom House,
King's Lynn**

places might well lead into an enquiry into the work of the local gilds (whose armorial bearings banners and shop signs provide starting points for painting and model-making).

Towns which once enjoyed, or still enjoy, something of a specialist position in the economy offer material uniquely their own. One cannot go to Burnham-on-Crouch (Essex), for example, without being aware of the importance of ships or to Stratford-on-Avon without being aware of Shakespeare.

An appreciation of the individual character of a town is only gained by close personal aquaintance. When a town has a distinctive "flavour" it is useful to try to analyse its uniqueness so that comparisons can be made. The class from Liverpool, for example, would find it worthwhile to compare their city with Dunwich (Suffolk), once one of the most prosperous ports in England.

The urban scene has as much to offer to the teacher as Castle, Cathedral, pretty fishing village or mediaeval manor house. History is around us — whether our school overlooks the ruins of a Norman keep or an industrial wasteland.

All we need to do is to learn how to look for it.

taken down as required. The merchants and traders eventually built houses on their 'work sites', thus defining many of the street lines which we follow today. Even the names remain with roads, streets, ways and alleys named after such things as milk, gold, fish, bread, silver, madder, saffron and leather. It is interesting to note that some trade streets required little space because although the merchandise was valuable it had little bulk (gold, silver) and comparatively few merchants handling it. Other merchants required much more space because the goods they sold had great bulk and little value (e.g. corn chandlers). The old established pattern of streets often remains to this day. Street names and market

UNIT 4
Roads

We cannot travel far without meeting a road or a trackway or a path of some sort and I suppose it is because roads have an inbuilt fascination that they play such a prominent part in the literature of childhood. Try to recall all the folk stories in which the hero sets off along the King's Highway to seek his fortune. It was on a road that Jack swopped his mother's cow for magic beans, that Whittington heard bells, that the three little pigs met the men with straw and sticks and bricks and that an unfortunate old lady lost her petticoats. It was also on a road that the Emperor paraded his new clothes for all to see. But before we dismiss these examples as the whimsy of childhood, think too of all the other writers who have been affected by the "mystery of the road".

Laurie Lee* writes of "the traditional forces which sent many generations along this road", John Masefield† of "treading the rocky road of no reply to some immortal end", Robert Frost of the "two roads which diverged in a yellow wood", Christina Rossetti of the road which "winds uphill all the way", and Rudyard Kipling of the ghostly men and women who still ride along the road "closed seventy years ago". To our poets and writers we can add archaelogists like Ian Rodger, geologists like Dr. Rudge, mathematicians like Professor Borst who between them seem to present a fascinating case for suggesting that Christian churches were often built on pagan sites because by so doing old established "sight lines" were preserved. These sight lines linked hill beacon with hill beacon, so making it easy to travel along the pre-Roman trackways, at the same time forming a complicated communications lattice*.

For children the magic of the road will not be as academic as that of Professor Borst, but it will provide source material for much work in the classroom. The first questions to be asked are "Where does the road come from?" and "Where does it go to?" The immediate answer (the two nearest villages or towns) could be used as starting points for map work, and this in turn could lead to a detailed study of the Ordnance Survey map of the area. Has the road a Ministry of Transport Classification? Has it a number? What does the number mean?

This study could develop in any number of ways. If it is designed to relate road transport to modern industry, the nearest large road to the school could be used for a traffic count. Remember to take the count over the same period each day (say for a week) to obtain some base figures from which to work. For example the group in Plate 21 took a count over five school days of both North and South bound traffic between 09.45 – 10.00 and 15.15 and 15.30. Fifteen-minute counts taken at other times during the day were then related to these figures. The count was also broken down into the type of traffic using the road (lorry, bus, car, taxi, motorcycle). Needless to say the bus group had the least to do! The statistics so gained were pictorially represented – an area in which art and mathematics fuse quite admirably.

*As I walked out one May morning, *André Deutsch*.
†Grace before ploughing, *Heinemann*.

*See Megalithic Mathematics by Ian Rodger, *The Listener*, 27 November 1969.

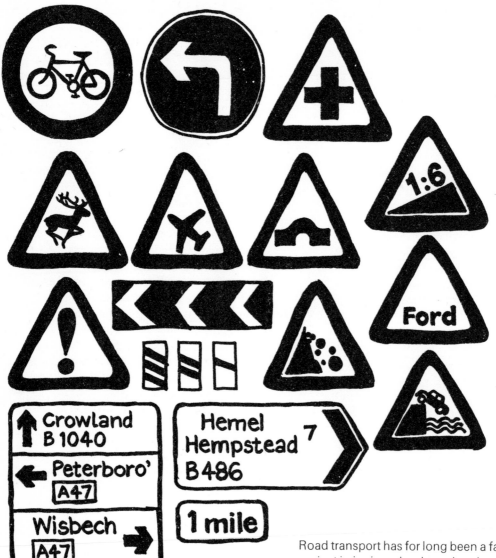

Road signs are another possible area of study. Apart from learning what the signs mean (important this, when so many young people ride "cycles"), one could also discuss with the group whether the signs are really satisfactory. Do they communicate meaning visually without words? Could they be improved? How? The final exercise of designing a set of signs for a new country (which has as yet no cars) is surprisingly challenging.

Road transport has for long been a favourite project in junior schools, embracing as it does over three thousand years of history. This is often treated in a straightforward developmental way. A lesson on the Celtic trackways is followed in rapid succession by others on Roman roads, the mediaeval wagon ways, the Elizabethan post roads and the Turnpikes, culminating in a film strip showing the construction of the latest motorway. Now lest it seem that I appear unhappy with this approach, I should add that it does have all the advantages of simplicity. It allows for a blanket coverage of almost everything from travelling by foot to the development of the wheel and the internal combustion engine. We can also show the road as an instrument of military power and as an essential part in the economic life of the community. We can compare the methods employed by Vespasian, Telford, Macadam and their latter-day counterparts.

Do we need, however, to consider the road near the school quite so abstractly? Can we not bring it to life in a historic sense, at the same time preserving all the teaching points which my analysis above does so deliberately? Let us assume, for example, that the road which passes the school joins the London–Dover Road. Who might have travelled along it? It was certainly part of Watling Street, and so would have felt the tread of legionaries between Rome and Londinium. Although it is conjecture that St. Augustine rode along it to Canterbury, Norman soldiers must have used the route regularly, as the fine keep and great cathedral at Rochester testify to this day. After the knights murdered Thomas countless pilgrims travelled from Dover and from London to worship at his shrine, Geoffrey Chaucer being but one of their number. The dissolution of the monasteries by Henry VIII did not halt the flow of travellers – merchants and bankers to the Low Countries, soldiers off to continental wars, cavaliers fleeing from Cromwell, Huguenots fleeing from France: Samuel Pepys to visit his Majesty's dockyards at Chatham, French Lords escaping from the terror, Charles Dickens to his house in Kent, English soldiers returning from Dunkirk. This particular method of approach is, of course, possible for almost any important road we care to choose – and if our school be close to one of the really ancient trackways (like Pedders Way in Norfolk) our study can be even richer than that described above.

In addition to writing descriptive and imaginative pieces about the road and the people who used it (supplemented with extracts from contemporary documents, diaries and novels) large wall friezes can also be made.

Join sheets of sugar paper longways to make a frieze 20" deep by 150" long and paint this in a pastel shade. This will form the road. Divide the class into small groups and invite each to draw a group of travellers to represent a different period in history – from pre-Roman times to the present day. The groups are worked on sugar paper (15" deep by 20" long) in crayon, oil pastel, paint or fabric scraps. These "travellers" are then cut out and mounted onto the paper frieze. The aim should be to make the travellers typical of their time – did they walk, ride, travel by litter, sedan chair, chariot, stage coach, mail coach, steam car, penny farthing, a "horseless carriage", a motor coach or a tram car? What did they wear? How long did it take to make a journey between two neighbouring towns?

The frieze could be supported by a picture map of the road, marrying together all its features from across the centuries. If this were attempted for the Great North Road, the Great West Road, Ermine Street*, the Fosse Way† or the road from Holyhead to Shrewsbury it would surely provide the average class of ten-year-olds with enough material for at least a year of environmental studies. (See Appendix 3).

Another way of looking at the road is to study the man-made structures upon it which are peculiar to this particular form of transport. There are signposts to be drawn, milestones to be rubbed. There might be a toll house or a

A Toll House

*York – Lincoln – Stamford – Huntingdon – London.
†Lincoln – Leicester – Cirencester – Bath – Axmouth.

coaching inn (see Unit 5), both of which provide for drawing, painting and research. How much did it cost to stay overnight in the Bull Inn in 1850? What was the toll on 1000 nails? *

In low-lying areas the road might be lined with ditches and dykes (as in the Fens), or it may have to cross a river by bridge or by ford . . . which would bring us to ask the sort of questions which occur again and again throughout this book.

* $\frac{1}{4}$d over the Monnow Bridge, Monmouth.

How old is it?
What is it made of?
Do we know who built it?
Are there any interesting stories about it?

While on the subject of bridges it might be found that some of the group would like to make this their particular study. Apart from providing much to draw and model, children could be encouraged to note certain things about each bridge they see. What is the shape of the cutwaters on the upstream and

A Clapper Bridge

A Packhorse Bridge
(Dob Park Bridge, Yorks.)

downstream face of the pillars ? What is the
shape of the arches ? Is there evidence that
there was onc e a ford or a ferry at this site ?
(The direction in which the road runs often
provides some indication). How many different
kinds of bridge can they make notes on ?
How many different types of material are used
in bridge building ? Why is wood used less
widely than brick, stone or iron ? How does a
suspension bridge remain stable ? What sorts
of bridges are to be found in docks ? What is
a clapper* bridge and how did it get its name ?
Why do packhorse bridges often have 'V'
shaped recesses ? The possibilities are endless.

On a less academic note, small children often
like to be taken for a short walk along a road
with which they are familiar simply so that
they can talk about it. In this case men mending
telephone wires or digging holes to look for
lost pipes come as a bonus to the understanding
infant teacher, as do unusual things seen
travelling along the road — like carthorses,
tractors, cranes, fire engines and steam engines.

John Stowe in his survey of London wrote
"The world runs on wheels with many whose
parents were glad to go on foot". Perhaps it is
appropriate that we should try to redress the
balance and encourage children, as the poet
Edward Thomas would have wished, "to love
roads".

*To save my readers much book searching — from the
Latin claperius — a pile of stones.

UNIT 5

Inns and taverns

The local pub has for centuries occupied a unique place in English social life. It goes without saying that although not all have managed to maintain their old-world charm in an age of one-armed bandits, piped music and bottled beer, a surprising number of them (even in town centres) have managed to preserve something of their past.

The most obvious thing for children to look at is the inn sign. This in itself serves as a reminder that in mediaeval times when few could read, all trades had a symbol of their own. Publicans, in fact, were compelled by a statute of Richard II enacted in 1393 to show a sign to facilitate the work of the king's ale taster as he moved, somewhat haphazardly I would imagine, from inn to inn sampling the quality of the brew. The sign provides the starting point for a whole range of activities in school. What does the local sign mean ? Is there a story behind it which will throw light on local history ? Is the design painted on a flat board, is it a model, or, far less common, is it mounted on a gallows which spans the road ? Inn signs can be classified in many ways, but the following headings should prove sufficient for all but the most inquisitive.

(a) **Royal** e.g. The Crown, The King's Head, The Rose, The Portcullis, The Castle, The Royal Oak (which commemorates Charles II's escape), The Rose and Crown (Elizabeth of York's marriage to Henry Tudor).

(b) **Baronial** e.g. The Red Lion (John of Gaunt), The Bear and Ragged Staff (Warwick), The Bankes Arms, The Swan (Duke of Buckingham).

(c) **People** Although the 'Duke of York' and the 'Marquis of Granby'* are the most popular characters for inn signs, the lives of Florence Nightingale, Christopher Wren, Amy Johnson, Charlie Chaplin and Napoleon are also remembered in this way.

(d) **Events** e.g. Trafalgar, Waterloo, Everest, The Two Lifeboats.

(e) **Mythological** e.g. The Dragon, The Mermaid, The Phoenix, The Unicorn.

(f) **Oddities** e.g. Who'd 'ave thought it ? The World turned upside down, Bunch of Carrots, Spyglass and Kettle, Labour in Vain.

(g) **Living Creatures** e.g. White Horse, Suffolk Punch, The Elephants, The Tiger, The Lion, The Eagle, The Duck, The Pheasant, The Cat, The Bee, The Trout.

*An army commander, the Marquis helped soldiers wounded in his campaigns to find places as landlords. Hence his popularity.

The Magpie
Little Stonham
Suffolk

Three-dimensional sign
(Sheepscombe, Gloucester)

Hanging sign (Wheldrake, nr. York)

(h) **Sports and Pastimes** e.g. The Bear (Bear baiting), Bird in Hand (Hawking) The Cock (Cock fighting), Dog and Duck (Shooting), Fox and Hounds (Hunting), Jolly Fishermen (Angling), The Cricketers, The Starting Gate.

(i) **Travel** This is a particularly valuable group because it illustrates the slowly changing character of travel from mediaeval times to the present day.

(1) The Age of Pilgrimage. Religious signs are very common. The Bull (Bulla – monastic seal – lodging place for pilgrims), Crossed Keys* Adam and Eve, The Angel, St. George, St. Thomas of Canterbury, The Turks Head (the Crusades). "The Manor of God Begot" (Winchester) is even today mediaeval both in name and in character.

(2) The Age of Wool. Signs such as The Pack Horse, The Carter, The Waggon and Horses, The Woolpack, are often found along the main cross-country routes used by the waggoners carrying staple and cloth to the great ports of mediaeval England on the South and East Coasts (e.g. Dunwich, Yarmouth, Romney, Hythe).

(3) The Age of Turnpikes, e.g. The Tollgates, Halfway House, Journey's End.

(4) The Age of Coaching, e.g. Coach and Horses, Four in Hand, Horse and Groom.

(5) The Age of Steam, e.g. Great Eastern, The Locomotive, Railway Arms, The Rocket.

*Often near a church dedicated to St. Peter.

(j) **Occupations** e.g. The Wheatsheaf (corn chandlers), Three Tuns (brewers), Golden Fleece (wool merchants), The Plough (farmers).

The sign itself will inspire research. What does the sign mean ? Who was the person ? What was the event ? Whose shield ? If several inns are near the school then interesting comparisons can be made and a collection of signs built up. (Fathers will take a particular interest in this aspect of environmental study !)

The inn will also be worth looking at in several other ways. Among questions which children could try to answer are:–

(1) How old is the building ? How long has there been an inn on the site ?

(2) Is there anything peculiar about the building, e.g. has it a gallery ?

(3) Was it used for coaching ? Is there any visible evidence of coaches using the inn ? e.g. mounting blocks, stables (probably now disguised as garages) coaching bills or posters, coaching yard ?

(4) Has it any associations with famous people ? e.g. Dick Turpin,* Queen Elizabeth I, or particular events or happenings in our history e.g. smugglers inns like Jamaica Inn (Bodmin Moor) or The Sussex Pad (Lancing).

(5) Are there any old engravings to be found at the local library or in local guide books ? Has the inn changed in appearance very much since the engraving was made ?

*If highwaymen is the theme read the group Alfred Noyes poem The Highwayman.

A Porte-cochère
(The New Inn, Gloucester)

In addition to making a model of the inn, art
work could be based upon making inn signs
(both actual and imaginary) and writing down
the story behind each sign. Because the designs
can take almost any form (from simple
geometric shapes to fine line drawings) there
is ample opportunity for the least artistic
children to achieve success. Work the design
on sugar or cartridge paper and mount on
straw board to prevent curling before display.

Outdoor work could, of course, include
drawings of the inn, as well as any interesting
parts of the building, e.g. doors, windows,
roofing

UNIT 6
Maps

The first accurate map of British roads was made by John Ogilby in 1675. Nearly one hundred years later, with the development of the turnpikes, Cary and Patterson began to publish their "Road Books" which were really guides to road travel. However, it was not until the Board of Ordnance were given the task of mapping England for military purposes in the 1780's that map making was taken really seriously.

The Ordnance Survey is, of course, now almost a national institution, and by the time they reach the age of eleven, the majority of children will have used the inch to the mile maps and tried to master the map symbols. Although the inch maps are those most commonly used in school, 2½" to the mile is far easier for young children to read. The 6" to the mile maps are even less well known, but they are almost essential if a detailed study of an area is being undertaken. If a larger scale is required Ordnance Survey maps are also available at a scale of 25 inches to a mile, and these are tremendously helpful if the group are studying the development of a small village community.

For studies which embrace several square miles (or if the rail and road routes between towns and villages are being plotted), Bartholomew's ½" to the mile maps are ideal. They are based upon Ordnance Survey maps of the area and show rather more detail than the touring maps sold by garages and petrol stations (though these too have a place).

Old maps of the area are also worth study if
they can be obtained. Even an Ordnance
Survey map made in the 1920's will clearly
show how the district has changed — some
buildings shown on the map will have
disappeared altogether, to be replaced,
perhaps, by rashes of semi-detached houses,
power stations or sewage works. It is worth
remembering that the British Museum Map
Room has a large collection of early maps, and
photostats can be purchased quite cheaply.

If it is wished to travel back in time (by map)
even further than the first Ordnance Survey
maps or the county maps of cartographers
such as Saxton, Speed and Norton, the
Stationery Office have also produced maps of
Ancient Britain, Roman Britain, Britain in the
Dark Ages and Monastic Britain.

UNIT 7

Churches

Our aim in following any environmental study programme should be to show children how to look, how to record their findings and where to find additional information. Thus it seems to me that initial enquiries should be based on something near at hand so that any number of visits may be made.

It has always seemed to me in this respect that the churches which dot our towns and villages are perhaps the richest starting point — and often the most neglected. Since the departure of the Romans in 410, the Church has played a vital and continuous part in the life and culture of our nation. It has inspired architects and builders, needlewomen (English ecclesiastical embroidery was once the most admired in Europe), craftsmen in silver, glass, wood and stone. Indeed it would be fair to say that it would be impossible to write a history of the Theatre, Literature, Music, Education, Social Reform, Medicine, Politics, Finance, Trade, Wool, Agriculture or Folk Lore and Customs without detailed reference to the part the church has played in its development.

Here then is our starting point. How can we develop it ? The questions we could ask the children are almost limitless, but broadly speaking they might range under the following headings (bearing in mind that the more experienced the children are in this sort of research, the more difficult the questions can be).

(a) The Building. What is it made of ? Is the stone local or does it come from some distance from the church ? Have bricks or tiles been used in addition to or instead of stone ? This might lead to the discovery that some stone was quarried near by, some obtained from famous British quarries (e.g Purbeck, near Swanage, Dorset) whilst some was imported from abroad.* There might also prove to be a link with pre-Christian times. The nave of St. Albans Abbey, for example, contains visible traces of tile taken from the site of the nearby Roman city of Verulamium.

(b) The roof. Is it made from slate, tile, stone, thatch or wood ? If thatch has been used is there any equipment for putting out roof fires ? (Many parish churches keep rudimentary fire-fighting equipment at the west end of the building. For example, the little church at Bere Regis, Dorset, has two "thatch hooks" for removing blazing straw).

(c) How old is the building ? When was the church built ? Can we tell anything from the style of architecture employed ? I don't think that one need bother small children with the finer points of Transitional, William and Mary and Regency, but a simple breakdown of period would be of value to them, particularly as their study develops and embraces civil and military architecture. A wall chart could be built up using the following headings; with spaces left for children to record information as they obtain it:

*Some churches and cathedrals are faced in Caen stone, quarried in Normandy, and brought to England as ballast in merchant ships. Caen stone was also used for the White Tower, London.

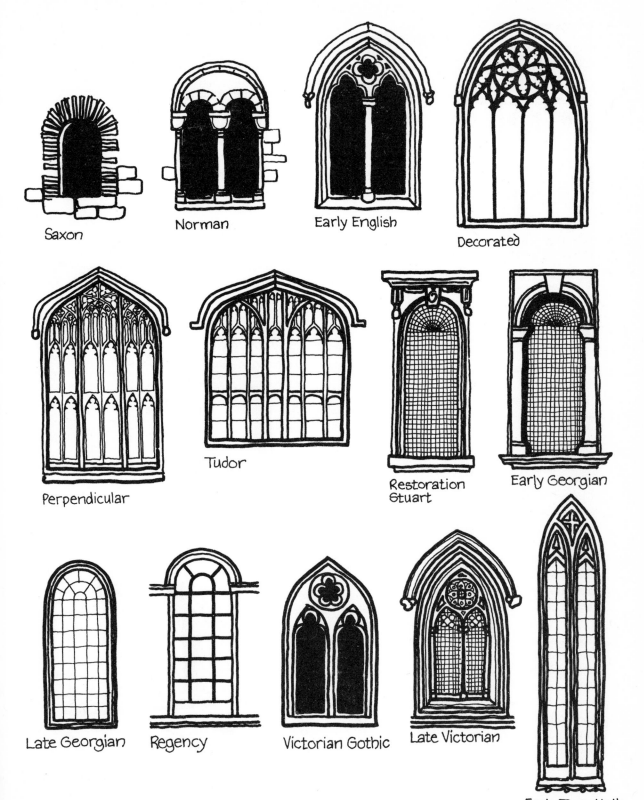

Saxon

Norman

Early English

Decorated

Perpendicular

Tudor

Restoration
Stuart

Early Georgian

Late Georgian

Regency

Victorian Gothic

Late Victorian

Early Twentieth
Century

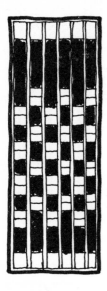

Contemporary

has a heraldic link with the mother priory of the Order of St. John of Jerusalem, Clerkenwell, London).

(e) What is the church plan ? A study of architectural terms will of necessity require the group to describe where particular things may be found. Thus, nave, tower, transepts, aisles, sanctuary, chapel will need to be introduced very early in the project. Even eight-year-olds should be able to follow a simple plan, and a duplicated sheet would more than repay the effort of production. In this connection there are many possible links with mathematics — width, length, height of nave, tower, spire. The Almighty will surely not be too upset at being used for estimation !

Saxon	(pre 1066)
Norman	(1066 – 1190)
Early English	(1160 – 1300)
Decorated	(1270 – 1350)
Perpendicular	(1350 – 1580)
Jacobean	(1600 – 1712)
Georgian	(1700 – 1820)
Victorian	(1830 – 1900)
Twentieth Century	

(d) Are there any interesting architectural features ? Initially the teacher will need to guide the children to look for certain things — for a squint, sedilia or misericord. Gradually, however, one should try to look beyond the obvious — to decorations (billet, chevron, cable, dog tooth, tablet) roof bosses, corbels, gargoyles, windows and vaulting. Individual children could be encouraged to look for particular things and report to the group on their findings. Windows and bosses are particularly interesting topics which will repay detailed study as they often feature local legends, commemorate events or record (through coats of arms and heraldic devices) the church's association with powerful benefactors, royalty, as well as other ecclesiastical bodies. (The church of St. Botolph, Boston, Lincolnshire, for example,

Piscina

Sedilia

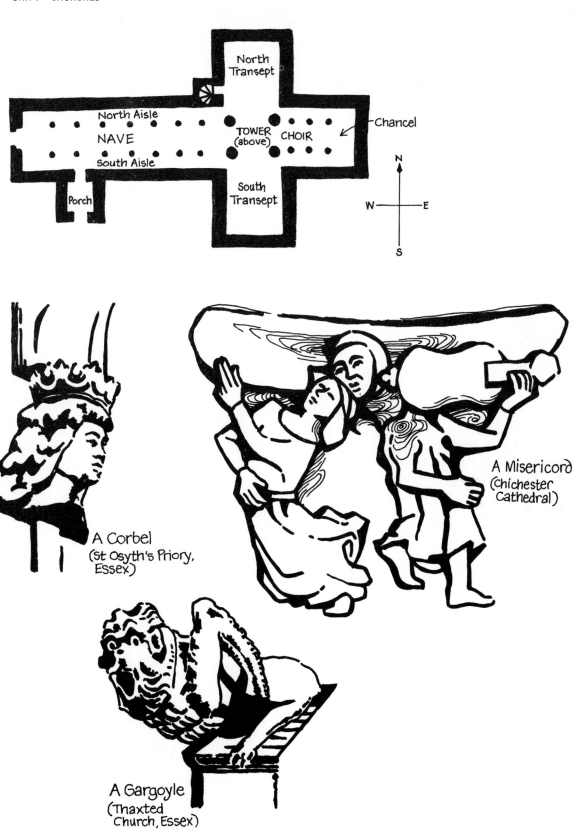

North Transept

North Aisle

NAVE

TOWER (above)

CHOIR

Chancel

South Aisle

South Transept

Porch

N

W — E

S

A Corbel
(St Osyth's Priory, Essex)

A Misericord
(Chichester Cathedral)

A Gargoyle
(Thaxted Church, Essex)

(f) What church furniture is of particular interest? Here one can range over a whole host of items – as varied as one's own interests.* The carving on pews and choir stalls (often misericords paint a remarkable picture of life in mediaeval England) altar frontals, credence tables, communion rails, pulpits, hour glasses, kneelers (often rich with tapestried pictures), silver plate and clocks are but a few of the possible subjects for discussion and research. I remember a tough nine-year-old boy holding a chalice presented to Wells Cathedral by Queen Elizabeth I and remarking "Now I've touched what a dead queen held. She knew Drake too!" Another group were fortunate to see (at different times) the five clocks built in the 14th century by Peter Lightfoot – the most famous of which is in Wells Cathedral. This achievement they remembered with pride, somewhat dashed when one of the children later enquired of a guide at the Palace of Westminster whether he had also been responsible for designing Big Ben.

(g) Are there any written accounts connected with the church? Most old churches can boast continuous records dating back to the regulations of Henry VIII's Vicar General in 1538, which required that every parish priest should keep a register of weddings, christenings and burials. Though difficult for young children to follow, lists can still be impressive. The registers at All-Hallows-by-the-Tower, London EC, for example, clearly show how deaths increased during the summer of 1665, the year of the plague.

(h) Are there memorials or brasses of interest? Effigies of people provide the best reason for using the church as a starting point for environmental studies. The effigies represent *people,* who lived, married, raised families, went to war, left bequests for the poor, died in and around the very place that the children themselves are studying. Though dead they somehow bring the past to life, illustrating the changes of fashion over the centuries – dress, armour, hairstyle, ornament – more effectively than any history book. Even the tombs themselves reflect changes in taste and fashion, developing from the flat twelfth-century slab to the sophisticated grandeur of the richly coloured life-size figure (with canopy, armorial bearings and family motto) of Stuart days. After the grotesquely dressed statues used to commemorate politicians, soldiers and explorers of the nineteenth century, it is worth noting, with relief, that the wheel of fashion has now turned full circle and we are back, once more, to the simpler tastes of the Plantagenets!

While on the subject of tombs, it is worthwhile to encourage children to look for examples which are unusual or not typical of their period. Thus there are few mediaeval tombs which show husband and wife holding hands, though whether this stems from a cynical view of marriage or a desire on the part of the craftsman concerned to obtain symmetry in his design, I am not sure. Then there are tombs of quixotic people, as at Wimborne Minster in Dorset, of a man who wanted to be buried half in the ground and half out of it, half in church and half out of it – and was!

Rubbings can be taken of brasses and tombstones with wax crayon or heelball on detail paper (the resist process described on Page 29 being used to add variety to the children's work). Drawings should be supported by some research on the life and times of the people buried beneath. This might result in the discovery of odd contradictions to the history books. Was it Dr. Jenner who discovered the relevance of the link between cowpox and smallpox or was it one Benjamin Jesty, a Dorset farmer, whose tombstone in Worth Matravers church yard claims that he, not Jenner, pioneered vaccination?

*At St. Mary the Virgin, Bishops Canning, Wiltshire, there is a meditation seat. Useful both for tired staff and noisy pupils.

Even the manner of the deaths of the inmates is sometimes of interest. Apart from shipwrecks and similar disasters, the history of England is liberally sprinkled with political executions, and although St. Peter ad Vincula (Tower of London) is particularly rich in this respect, many of our smallest churches contain the remains of the odd knight who did not please his temporal master and was therefore hastened heavenwards.

The list of rectors, while not proving conclusively disasters in the village, often serves to indicate periods of unrest. In the church of St. Sampson, Cricklade, Gloucestershire, for example, the living changed hands five times during the period 1348/49 when the Black Death was at its height. Does this suggest that the plague hit the area severely – or have the figures no significance at all ?

On a less aristocratic level, the plague of 1665 is still remembered at Eyam in Derbyshire where 259 of the villagers died, a service being held to mark the fact on the last Sunday in August every year. Most of the villagers were buried in the churchyard. At Upwell St. Peter, Cambridgeshire a plaque reads "In memory of 67 individuals of various age and either sex who, in the short period from June 21st – August 13th AD 1832, died in this rectory of Asiatic cholera, a frightful and previously unknown disease in this country".

Death is perhaps not a thing to concentrate on – but the examples given above do provide useful source material for a lively health education programme.

(i) To whom is the church dedicated ? A quick glance at the county list in the Appendix will suggest that by far the most popular saint for this purpose is St. Mary. However, the more unusual dedications serve our purpose better. Broadly speaking we could classify dedications as follows:

(1) Biblical. New Testament apostles. (St. Michael, St. Paul, St. Peter etc.)

(2) Historical figures (e.g. St. Margaret of Scotland, St. Chad, St. Felix, St. Cuthbert, St. David, St. Germanus).

(3) Legendary figures (St. George, St. Christopher).

(4) Local Saints (e.g. St. Adhelm in Dorset, Gloucestershire and Wiltshire, St. Edmund in Suffolk, St. Swithin at Winchester).

(5) Saints associated with particular crafts, professions and callings (e.g. churches dedicated to St. Nicholas, the patron saint of sailors, are often near the sea). Others in this category include St. Crispin (bootmakers), St. Giles (hospitals), St. Tibba (falconers).

This still leaves opportunity for a great deal of local research. In my short appendix I include churches dedicated to St. Wendreda, St. Morwenna, St. Mary de Haura, St. Wilfred, St. Beuna, St. Wulfram, St. Nectan, St. Hardulph, St. Cressian, St. Protus, St. Hyacinth, St. Candida, St. Wystan and St. Ronald. My guess would be that the majority of these have particular local associations, and if this is the case, it would be worth while looking in the area for further evidence, e.g. a holy well (the well of St. Neot at St. Neots, Cornwall), other nearby churches with similar dedications or windows depicting the saint during his lifetime.*

(j) Is there any visible evidence of the church being used for purposes other than religious services ? Most churches suffered somewhat during the Protectorate and, if local legend is to be believed, Cromwell stabled his horse in almost every church in England. This temporary use of the building, however, though of interest, is not what I would list

*One or two churches have no dedication. This is usually because they were first brought into use during the Commonwealth.

under this heading. Some churches had a tower built for defence (at St. Mary's, Swanage, the lower part may well have been a fortification against the Danish raiders during Alfred's reign). St. Botolph's great lantern tower was used by generations of seamen as a land mark to guide them into Boston harbour (and it probably still serves the same purpose). This church also has a school room (now a chapel) and a parvise (now a library containing manuscripts dating from c. 1150).

(k) Has the church a museum or collection of documents which give further evidence of the growth and development of the community it was built to serve ? This is a far-ranging question which in some cases will result in little, but in others provide source material for a year's work. As one might expect, the most comprehensive collections are in the bigger churches (those at Westminster Abbey and Durham Cathedral being particularly extensive). But many churches have indentures and old seals, and chained bibles are not as rare as one might think, while at Mendlesham (in Suffolk) the church was also used as the armoury for the parish.

(l) Is there anything of interest outside the church ? While some children explore the inside of the building its immediate surroundings often provide interesting additional information. On the exterior of the church itself the following might be seen:

Gargoyles
Tympanum (carving over doorways)
Stepped and flying buttresses
Weathercocks (not always a cockerel, sometimes a fish, sometimes a decorated banner. Some weathercocks "sing" in the wind)
Sanctuary knocker (Durham Cathedral has the most famous one)
Church clock (a number of church clocks have mechanical jacks)

The churchyard might have a lych gate, stocks (as at Shoreditch Parish Church, London and Ottery St. Mary, Devon) a separate Bell Tower (as at Chichester Cathedral), or an unusual early cross (the church at Halton, Lancashire boasts of one dating from Viking times while St. Columb Major, Cornwall, has a Celtic wheel cross of c. 800 AD).

The sundial, however, provides perhaps the most useful teaching material. Many old churches have a scratch dial (usually situated near the South doorway). Here the hour lines are scratched in the stonework and the gnomon (pointer) was a stick or metal rod. Often the nine o'clock line is deeper than the rest of the scratches because this was the usual time for Mass. Vertical sundials might also be found on church towers (St. Mary the Virgin, Putney, London and St. Mary, Cricklade, Gloucestershire both have good examples of this). Some churchyards also have the flat table sundial we are accustomed to seeing in gardens and parks. Returning to school, experiments with shadows (sun clocks) lead naturally to mathematics based on time.

10th century Celtic Cross

GLOSSARY

Aisle
Part of church, on either side of nave or chancel.

Apse
Recess at the end of a building; usually semi-circular.

Boss
A decoration at the junction of two or more ribs of a vault.

Chancel
Eastern part of church.

Chantry (chapel)
A special chapel set aside for regular masses for a specific person or persons.

Clerestory
The side wall of the nave above the aisle roof. Usually pierced with windows.

Credence (table)
A table for holding the vessels of the mass.

Crossing
The space where the east-west axis of the church is crossed.

Gargoyle
Stone waterspout by the north-south transepts.

Misericords
Hinged wooden seats, usually found in the choir.

Piscina
A small hand basin with a drain beside an altar. Used to cleanse sacramental vessels.

Pyx
Above the mediaeval altar was often a canopy. From this hung a box containing the sacrament for administration to the sick and dying.

Reredos
Ornamental screen at the back of an altar.

Sedilia
Seats for officiating clergy carved into the south wall of the sanctuary.

Squints
Holes pierced through the wall on one or both sides of the chancel arch to give sight of the high altar. Also known as Hagioscopes.

Transept
Transverse part of a cruciform church set at right angles to the east-west axis.

Tympanum
The filling of the arch of a Norman doorway: in classical architecture, the triangular space enclosed by the sides of a pediment.

Water stoup
A recessed basin near the porch for holding holy water.

UNIT 8
Cathedrals

Provided the children have made some study of their local church they should have no difficulty in understanding that a cathedral is little more than a parish church writ large. Architecturally it has been designed for the same purpose (i.e. the observance of religious rites) and one should expect to find certain similarities.

There are, however, certain points which will have to be made. The Cathedral is the seat of the Bishop of the diocese – and so all cathedrals have a Bishop's throne. Moreover, since many of our cathedrals were built long before the Reformation, they often contain traces of the monastic foundations from which they evolved. Thus there might be a Chapter House (that at Wells is superb), cloisters (the cloisters at Gloucester boast both a lavatorium where the monks washed and the recess in which they hung their towels), or other outbuildings (at Peterborough these include the Abbot's and Prior's lodgings and a number of gateways; at Ely the sacristy and almonry as well as a 14th-century barn).

I have always found it worthwhile to write to the Cathedral I propose to visit so that, if possible, a short guided tour or introductory talk can be arranged (the Dean's Verger usually deals with these matters). It is important to indicate the age of the children making up the party and often useful (from the guide's point of view) if some suggestions are made as to the type of information it is hoped to obtain. Thus it would be possible to tour Southwark Cathedral and simply talk about people – John Harvard. Cardinal Beaufort, Edmund and William Shakespeare, John Gower, Philip Massinger, Edward Alleyn and Launcelot Andrewes. At Westminster Abbey* one could concentrate on Kings and Queens, while Peterborough (after a series of unfortunate fires and collapses) provides sufficient material for a history of early architectural styles. (There is a mediaeval winch in the roof above the nave which was actually used during the cathedral's construction.)

The Abbot's Kitchen, Glastonbury

*Not a Cathedral but a royal peculiar. Used here for illustrative purposes only!

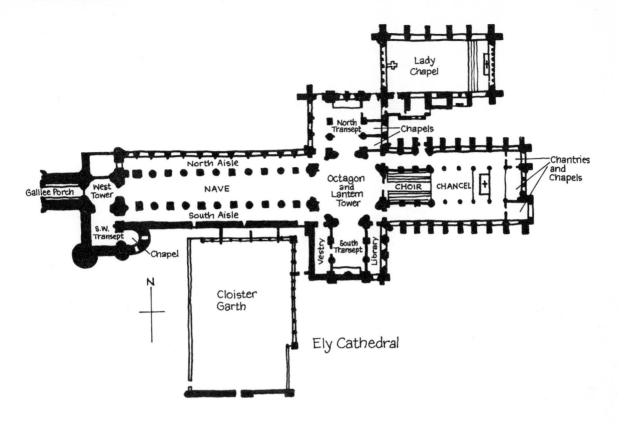

Ely Cathedral

A letter requesting help invariably means that additional facilities are made available. These might include a climb to the top of the tower or a private viewing of some of the Cathedral treasures. Again it is wise to make the guide aware of the children's interests. Ecclesiastical embroidery, which could be followed up at school by collage work of all types, appeals to most girls, while silver plate has a universal fascination. (At Lincoln, for example, there is a treasury sponsored by the Worshipful Company of Goldsmiths and Silversmiths; a group I took to Wells were allowed to handle an exquisite 16th-century paten and chalice.) At Exeter the library can be visited and as it contains the "Exon Doomsday" such an opportunity should not be missed.

The Cathedrals at Coventry, Liverpool and Guildford could be looked at from quite a different viewpoint, particularly if the children are of secondary age. In these buildings attempts have been made to relate the Christian message to present-day society, contemporary artists, designers and craftsmen employing contemporary techniques to modern materials. *One has only to think of the impressive west window of Coventry with its etched angels and the great circular lantern of the Roman Catholic Cathedral of Christ the King in Liverpool to appreciate how effectively this philosophy is being applied.

*Dean Hussey has introduced contemporary art with telling effect to Chichester Cathedral. There is a screen woven to a design of John Piper. A picture by Graham Sutherland provides focal point for the South Aisle and some of the altar furniture and the nave pulpit are of beaten aluminium. As Dean Hussey remarked on TV recently "All art in its time is contemporary".

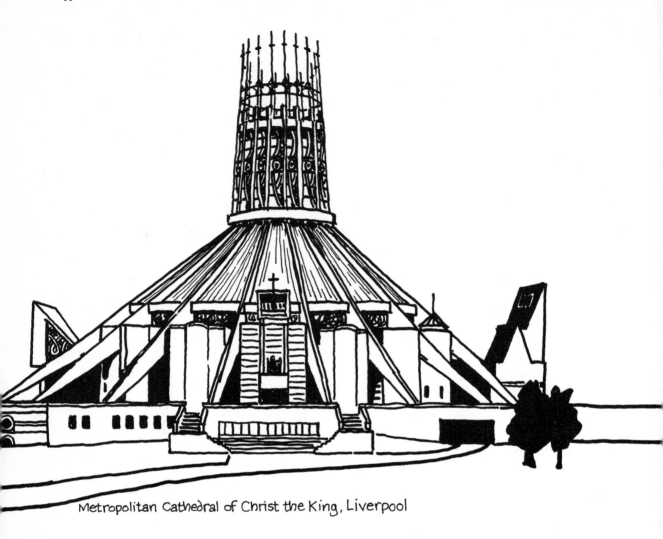

Metropolitan Cathedral of Christ the King, Liverpool

During the visit it might be necessary to introduce a few more architectural terms. Chantry Chapels, for example, can be seen in many parish churches, but for sheer quantity we need to go to the mediaeval foundations of Canterbury, York, Lichfield, Worcester, Salisbury, Winchester or Norwich. It is also more likely that these great churches will have undercrofts or crypts. The atmosphere evoked by the claustrophobic dimness of Rochester is in strange contrast with the airy lightness of Wren's St. Paul's.

It might also prove of worth to try to link the cathedral with its immediate surroundings, particularly where the town has historical significance. A town in the Middle Ages was often based upon a very simple planning formula—"a square for God and a square for Man". Thus ecclesiastic and commercial interest could live side by side without undue friction, both groups being protected by the city wall and perhaps a castle. Do street names suggest that in the past certain areas enjoyed ecclesiastical patronage (e.g. Crucifix Lane, Abbey Walk, Monastery Street, Bishops Place) while others were more devoted to trade and commerce (e.g. Madder Market, Exchange Street, Corn Hill) ?

The visit should, of course, provide material for follow-up work. This might include maps and plans, notes, tape recordings, pictures and rubbings. The expense of buying 35 mm transparencies is worthwhile since they can contribute much to recreating the atmosphere of the building on return to school.

Abbeys, Monasteries and Priories

The majority of our cathedrals can trace their history back to pre-Reformation times, and it is therefore advisable to give children the opportunity of visiting at least one of them before attempting to interest the group in the many abbey ruins which dot the countryside. The cathedral building should give an idea of the skill of the mediaeval craftsmen — difficult to grasp when looking at sad (though well-kept) piles of fallen masonry.

It would also be helpful if some picture could be built up of the life of the monks and nuns, and for this the following information will prove of use:

All the various foundations may be described as "religious houses". A house of monks was called a monastery, that of nuns a nunnery. However, a monastery or nunnery could also be an Abbey, provided an Abbot or Abbess was a resident member of the community. If, however, the religious house did not have Abbey status it was called a Priory (run by a Prior or Prioress). In this case it was usually an offshoot from another Abbey and dependent upon it. In addition to these the houses of the itinerant friars were usually called friaries and those of the Carthusian monks were known as Charterhouses.

Personally I would not bother overmuch about the particular differences between the orders (except to stress that the friars were wanderers and to mention that the Carthusians* did not follow the typical monastic day since (apart from certain communal meals and services) they prayed,

*Only relevant if a Charterhouse is being visited.

ate and slept in solitude. Dress varied, of course, from order to order, but again the task of the teacher is not to fill each child with a plethora of tedious detail but rather to make a way of life come alive. A brief description of the habit (with colour variations) should suffice, though this allows children who show particular interest in costume to follow a study of their own, supporting written work with applique pictures, felt collage or by dressed dolls (see Appendix 3).

The question of why people entered the monastic orders might be raised by the more thoughtful children. Alfred the Great, describing the society of his time, wrote "There are those who fight, those who till, those who pray". The need for this third group is clearly put in *Abbeys* by R. Gilyard-Beer (H.M.S.O. 1959). "Early monasticism appealed to the mediaeval mind as a living example of successful organisations based on Christian principles. But as the centuries passed and the general level of civilisation rose the monasteries lost their dominant position as repositories of learning, models of organised community life, leaders in architectural and artistic enterprise and sources of education".

It is impossible to state exactly how the monk spent his day. This would vary according to the Order and each house would have individual peculiarities. Moreover special Feast Days and Holy Days required particular observances. However, children are fascinated by the following basic timetable:

2.30 am	Rise. Psalms and Prayers
	Nocturn (the first service)
	Mattins
Dawn	Prime
	Reading in the Cloister
	Ablutions
8.00 am	Terce
	Morrow Mass
9.00 am	Meeting in the Chapter House (to plan day-to-day life of the monastery)

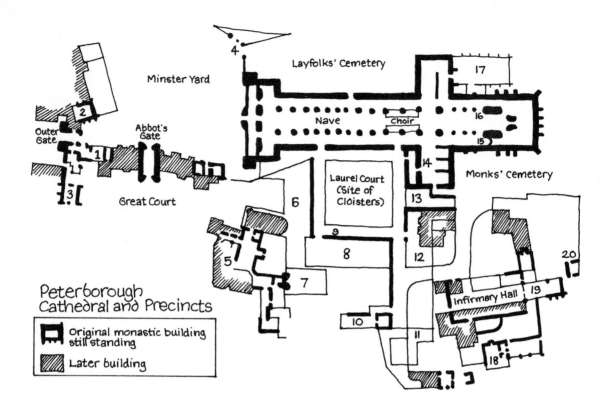

Peterborough Cathedral and Precincts

- ▣ Original monastic building still standing
- ▨ Later building

1 Abbot's Prison
2 Chapel
3 King's Lodging
4 Prior's Gate
5 Abbot's Lodging now Bishop's Palace
6 Site of Abbot's Hall & Cellarer's Building
7 Site of Monks' Kitchen
8 Site of Monks' Refectory
9 Monks' Washing Places & Towel Cupboards
10 Little Dorter & Misericord

11 Reredorter
12 Site of Monks' Dormitory
13 Site of Chapter House
14 Site of Saxon Church
15 Mary Queen of Scots' Burial Place
16 Catherine of Aragon's Burial Place
17 Site of Lady Chapel
18 Hostry Buildings now Deanery
19 Infirmary Chapel
20 Infirmarer's Lodging

10.00 am   Reading
           Work
Noon   Sext
           High Mass
           None
 2.00 pm   Meal in the refectory or frater (often
           eaten in silence, a brother reading
           from the Scriptures or Church
           Fathers)
           Reading
           Work
 5.00 pm   Vespers
           Light refreshment
 6.00 pm   Compline
 7.00 pm   Retire to the Dorter to sleep.

The Cellarer	Stores, food, wine, ale
The Chamberlain	The monks' sleeping quarters Clothing and footwear
The Fraterer	The dining room The lavatorium
The Hospitaller	Hospitality for guests
The Infirmarian	The hospital
The Kitchener	The kitchens
The Novice Master	The education of novitiates
The Precentor	Church Services Music
The Sacristan	Vestments, church plate

The work which the brothers would follow was very varied. Apart from the Cistercian houses, servants performed most of the manual tasks, giving the brothers the opportunity to concentrate on activities requiring a greater degree of skill — teaching the novices, illuminating the scriptures, keeping the abbey records and accounts, carving ,painting, tending the sick, preparing the music (in fact everything which has to be done to ensure that a large community lives together happily, from buying food and wine, mending the towels and bed covers to the supply, at three-weekly intervals, of hot water for head shaving).

Here again one need not go too deeply into the various offices within the monastery, but as children are interested in people and as the work which people do largely determines the way they spend their lives, a list of offices is also of use:—

The Abbot	The Head, elected by the monks themselves
The Prior	The Abbot's deputy
The Sub Prior	The Prior's assistant
The Almoner	The care of the local poor

Background detail of this sort should be further supplemented by film strips. Educational Productions, Wakefield, Yorks, market a series of excellent strips illustrating monastic building, monastic life and monastic achievement, (e.g. book illustration), pictures (Pictorial Education) and extracts from literature (Bede *A History of the English church and people,* Helen Waddell *Abelard,* Chaucer, *The Canterbury Tales,* and *The little flowers of St. Francis).* Music should not be ignored. Records of plainsong chant are widely available, and though not recommending that young juniors should listen to the Mass in its entirety, I have found that a short excerpt does much to evoke something of a long gone age.

A visit to an Abbey ruin will require a considerable amount of preparation and one might well ask whether the whole operation is worth while. My experience would suggest that it is. Once the pattern of life within the pattern of a building has been understood, the children can quickly relate particular functions to particular parts of the ground plan. (All monastic remains in the care of the Ministry of Public Building and Works are very clearly marked). Arches, pillars, arcades, fallen corbels and bosses provide inspiration for drawing. Occasionally the visit can spark off all manner of follow-up work. The Abbot's kitchen at Glastonbury, for example, with its brilliantly conceived roof built to allow the air to circulate freely, led to a long discussion with a group of ten-year-olds on the properties of heat. The same class contained several children who had heard of King Arthur. Here, at Glastonbury, legend has it that he is buried with his Queen. Legend, romance, fiction, fact? As teachers, part of our task should be to make children aware that fact and fiction, romance and legend have sometimes to be unravelled if we are really to understand the past.

If the group are particularly interested in craft, a visit may also reveal much information on tools which were used as well as the way things were made (e.g. ceramic dishes, glassware, knives, carpentry tools, agricultural implements – perhaps even a kiln).

Chapels

This brief section on churches, cathedrals and abbeys would be incomplete without some reference to other religious sects. Many small towns and villages can boast a Baptist chapel going back to Cromwellian days – and these often have associations as rich and meaningful as any of our churches. The stumbling block, for our purpose, lies in the austere nature of their interiors, (often lacking in both monuments and plaques).

If in London, however, a visit to Wesley's House and Chapel (City Road E.C.) will do something to redress the balance.

NOTABLE ENGLISH CATHEDRALS

Bath Abbey Somerset

Bristol Cathedral Gloucestershire

Canterbury Cathedral Kent

Carlisle Cathedral Cumberland

Chester Cathedral Cheshire

Chichester Cathedral Sussex

Coventry Cathedral Warwickshire

Durham Cathedral Co. Durham

Ely Cathedral Cambridgeshire

Exeter Cathedral Devon

Gloucester Cathedral Gloucestershire

Guildford Cathedral Surrey

Lichfield Cathedral Staffordshire

Lincoln Cathedral Lincolnshire

Liverpool Cathedral Lancashire

London

St. Paul's Cathedral London E.C.4

St. George's Cathedral (RC) London, S.E.1

Southwark Cathedral London S.E.1

Westminster Cathedral (RC) London S.W.1

Norwich Cathedral Norfolk

Oxford Cathedral Oxfordshire

Peterborough Cathedral Huntingdonshire

Ripon Cathedral Yorkshire

Rochester Cathedral Kent

St. Albans Cathedral Hertfordshire

Salisbury Cathedral Wiltshire

Southwell Cathedral Nottinghamshire

Wells Cathedral Somerset

Winchester Cathedral Hampshire

Worcester Cathedral Worcestershire

York Minster Yorkshire

UNIT 9
Castles

Of all the places that we can take children to explore, perhaps the most exciting is the castle. Now let me make it clear from the start that by "castle" I mean earthworks (like Maiden Castle in Dorset) and Roman Forts (like Porchester) as well as great stone fortifications like Edinburgh, Harlech and Deal. By doing this I am aware that I am deliberately inviting criticism from learned historians who recently took our map-makers to task for using this term to embrace everything from prehistoric hill forts to pseudo-Gothic shams.* However, bearing in mind that young children are hardly likely to be able to appreciate the niceties so beloved by experts, I would suggest that we could begin by looking at the castle, hillfort, fortified house, nearest to the school in which we teach.

*According to B. H. St. J. O'Neil, sometime Chief Inspector of Ancient Monuments for the Ministry of Public Buildings and Works, "a castle was a private fortress of a king or noble constructed of earth or stone erected after the Norman Conquest".

Maiden Castle,
Dorchester

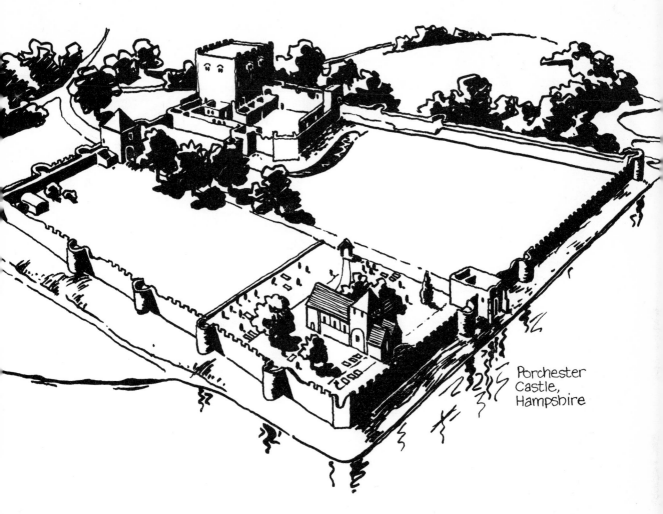

Porchester
Castle,
Hampshire

The first question which would need to be asked would probably be about the people who built it. When did they live? What did they look like? Why did they build it where they did? What materials did they use? When was the castle last lived in? The answers immediately give something of an insight into the period under consideration.

Let us examine some of the possible answers at length.

(a) **How old is the site?** This question will need to be phrased in such a way as to be pertinent to the children concerned in the study. Porchester, for example, is essentially Roman with considerable mediaeval additions;

Kenilworth dates from 1155 but its link with Elizabeth 1 and the masques which were held during her reign in John of Gaunt's "new" buildings will interest children far more than an analysis of crenellations and donjons. In other words we should be specific in our initial aim — most castle sites span the centuries and present far too much material for children to grasp on one visit.

(b) **Why was the site chosen?** Castles were built for a variety of reasons, most of which even young children can appreciate.

(1) To guard a pass, river valley, a shore or a river crossing, e.g. Dolwyddelan Castle, Caernarvonshire, Deal Castle, Kent.

Motte and Bailey

(2) To administer an area which has been conquered, e.g. Caernarvon Castle.

(3) As a refuge in troubled times, e.g. Borthwick Castle, Midlothian, which was entered by a doorway on the first floor; The Vicar's house, Corbridge, Northumberland.

In this connection older children might like to plot castles built during a particular period of history. The Edwardian castles of Wales are then seen as part of a far-seeing plan to subjugate the Welsh. On the other hand a castle sited like the one at Corfe (Dorset) merely controls a stretch of land (in this case the Isle of Purbeck) and little else.

(c) **What materials have been used to build the castle?** The earliest Norman Castles were built of wood — "an earthwork, surrounded by a moat crowned with a palisade enclosing a wooden tower"* (the motte).

*Castles in England and Wales (*Ministry of Public Buildings and Works*).

Nearby was often a banked and palisaded courtyard which sheltered household buildings (the bailey). These wooden castles were often rebuilt in stone (e.g. Castle Rising, Norfolk; Castle Hedingham, Suffolk; Rochester, Kent) but the initial earthworks are still visible and worth exploring. Examples of this type of earthwork are quite common throughout England and the border counties. Particularly fine examples are to be seen at Berkhamsted (Hertfordshire), Bolingbroke (Lincolnshire), Hen Dormen (Montgomery), Pickering (Yorkshire), and Lewes (Sussex).

The stone castles which developed from these primitive motte and bailey strongholds were of several types. The keep, for example, was built in stone at Colchester and in London during William's reign and some stone curtain walls (e.g. Richmond, Yorkshire) date from a similar period.

The materials used for castle building were often quarried locally, although some were

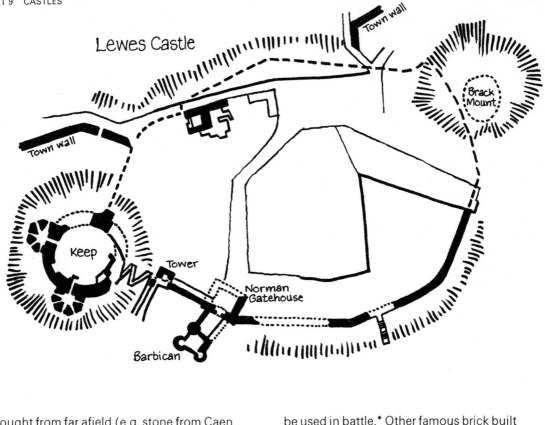

Lewes Castle

Town wall

Brack Mount

Town wall

Keep

Tower

Norman Gatehouse

Barbican

brought from far afield (e.g. stone from Caen was used for the White Tower, London). Looking at the stone is worthwhile. Castles aren't just a uniform dull grey (a fact that most illustrators of children's history books seem to ignore). Berkeley castle (Gloucestershire) is pink, Rougemont (Exeter, Devon) is dark red, Ashby de la Zouch (Leicestershire) is rich brown, Corfe (Dorset) is white. The stones reflect the resources of the locality and it might prove profitable to encourage children to list places where similar materials have been used (e.g. the church, the parish dovecot, cottages — often incorporating dressed stones removed from castles which were razed during the Civil War).

Brick was incorporated into some castles during the later Middle Ages, though as this period also marks the advent of gunpowder we could regard these buildings as little more than the final flowerings of a dying age. The keep at Tattershall (Lincolnshire) for example has an abundance of defensive paraphernalia, its purpose being to flatter its lord rather than be used in battle.* Other famous brick built castles may be seen at Hurstmonceux, Sussex, and Kirby Muxloe, Leicestershire.

(d) How did castles develop? The military lessons learned on the Crusades meant that castles began to be built in a new style. Round towers, for example, were stronger than square ones. They were less expensive on materials and far easier to roof. Militarily they were easier to defend, having no dead ground. The importance of the curtain walls was now appreciated, often being towered along their length. Particular attention was also given to the gatehouse which became by far the most impregnable part of the whole building (with portcullis, drawbridge and flanking towers), Beaumaris Castle, Anglesey, is the finest example of this type of castle in the British Isles.

*"A demonstration of arrogance on the part of a ruling class whose martial traditions required that they should house themselves in mansions where semblance of armed defence was preserved". (Castles in Britain by W. Douglas Simpson, published by Batsford, 1969).

Exploring a castle with children can be hair-raising. Assuming that there are two adults to 40 children, I have always found it wise to divide the group into two parties, each of which begins at a different part of the site. One adult can lead 20 children over the curtain walls and towers of a castle like Framlingham or Beaumaris – but double the number and the situation becomes unmanageable and positively dangerous.

Before a castle visit give the group some specific things to look for and make them aware of some of the basic architectural terms. I'm not sure that an eight-year-old needs to know that a crenellated wall was broken into solids (merlons) and voids (embrasures) or that a parapet walk was called an allure. However, I *do* think that a teacher who is responsible for boys of primary age will look foolish if he does not have some inkling of siege warfare –

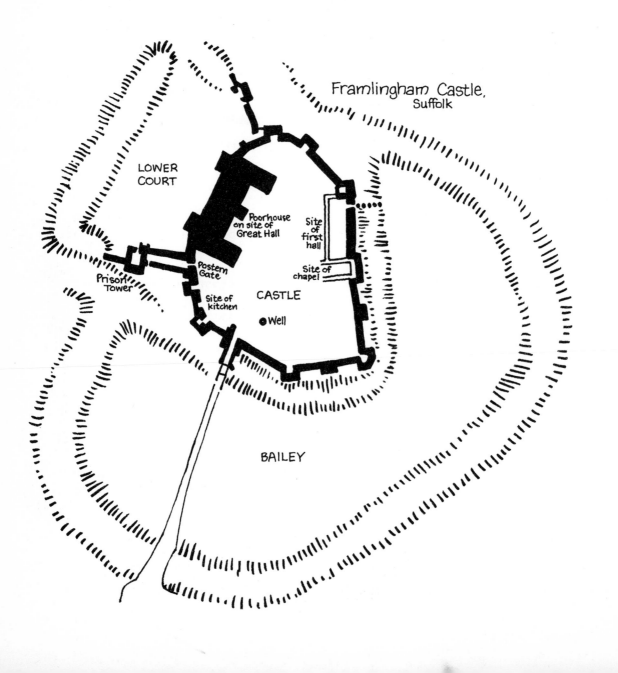

Framlingham Castle, Suffolk

LOWER COURT

Poorhouse on site of Great Hall

Site of first hall

Postern Gate

Site of chapel

Prison Tower

Site of kitchen

CASTLE

● Well

BAILEY

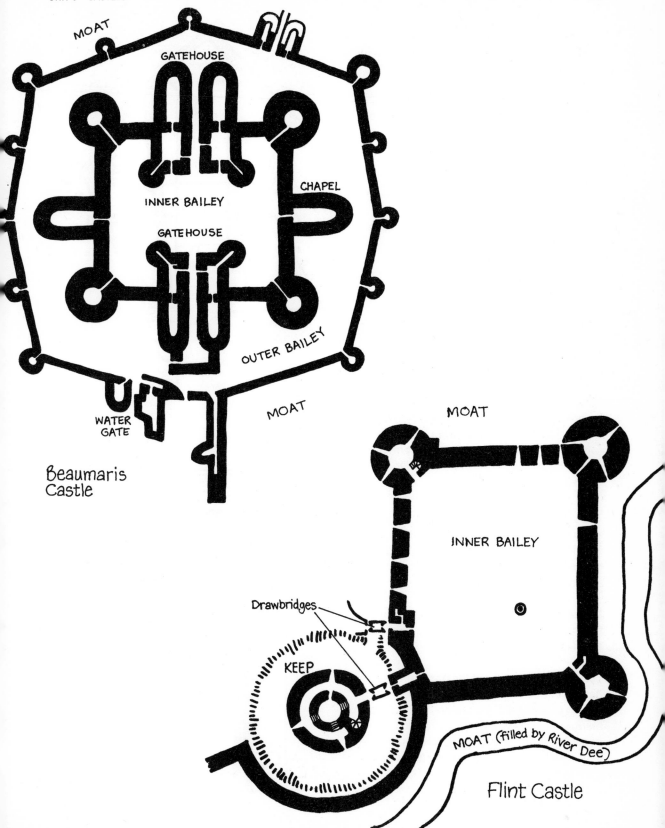

MOAT

GATEHOUSE

CHAPEL

INNER BAILEY

GATEHOUSE

OUTER BAILEY

WATER
GATE

MOAT

Beaumaris
Castle

MOAT

INNER BAILEY

Drawbridges

KEEP

MOAT (filled by River Dee)

Flint Castle

putlog holes, portcullis, murder holes (meurtrières), drawbridges, oubliettes and the like. On a less sinister note fireplaces, the Great Hall and the kitchens provide a rich source of material for sketching. Most castles also had a chapel and though few of them are as glorious as the one at Ludlow, the fact that they existed at all serves to emphasise the closeness of Church and State during this period of our History.

In this connection it is often worth while to visit the local church after visiting the castle to see if there are any obvious links between the two buildings. Sometimes the church contains the funeral banners of long dead local squires or the tombs of people who lived in the castle. If the tombs are of the effigy type (e.g. as at Ashby de la Zouch, Leicestershire) details of dress can be noted. Armorial bearings on pillars and roof bosses also provide material for subsequent research. The castle walls are also worth study. How thick are they ? What sort of windows (or loopholes) do they have ? Is the window a simple slit or does it incorporate a round hole (an oilette) ? Is the loophole in the form of a cross ? Has the wall any gun ports ? Do castle walls join the town ?

The well will also fascinate. At Dover, for example, where it is exceptionally deep, visitors can watch a lighted taper drop down the shaft. Children's comments on seeing this are rich indeed !

It is because castles have immediate appeal to young children that follow-up activities in the classroom can be so rewarding.

Let me examine some of the possibilities in detail. Written work could be linked to the history of the castle, the children's descriptions being supported with their own pencil, pen or pen and wash drawings. These "guidebooks in miniature" appeal particularly to those members of the group who do not enjoy picture-making on a large scale. Stories about

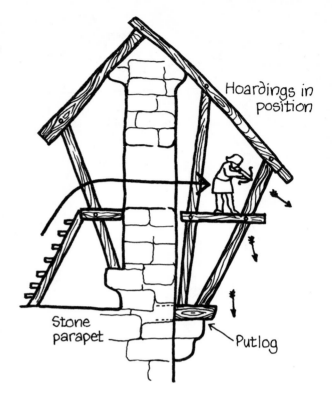

Hoardings in position

Stone parapet

Putlog

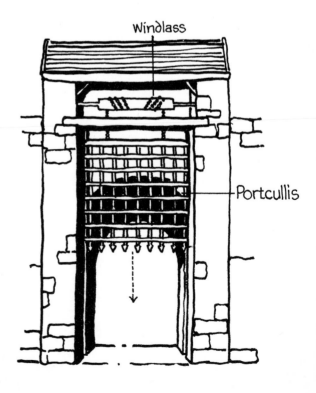

Windlass

Portcullis

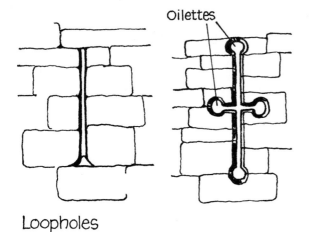

Oilettes

Loopholes

people who lived in the castle are often worth recording, and the fact that the incidents are macabre or bizarre seems to make it easier for children to retell them successfully. I am thinking here of stories like the ghost of St. Thomas a Becket who reappeared annually on his feast day to knock down a newly erected archway in the Tower of London with his crozier until a far-seeing Governor renamed the gateway after the Saint; or of the ghost of Henry VII who returns to the drawing room of Berkeley Castle to make sure that all the chairs face East as they did in his day when the room was a chapel. Even murders — Edward II at Berkeley, Richard II at Pontefract, Queen Mary at Fotheringhay — seem less horrifying with the passage of time (though personally I would not dwell overlong on political blood-letting).

Some well-preserved castles still have an atmosphere of their own which gifted children will be able to recapture in words — castles like Orford (Essex) whose very isolation conjures up ghostly horsemen hurrying across the marshes to the safety of its walls, or Castle Hedingham (Suffolk), nestling in a pretty valley, whose empty apartments lend themselves to fantasies of knights and their ladies at ease before the great fireplaces listening to the songs of some mediaeval troubadour. On an equally imaginative plane

the dungeons* are guaranteed to excite interest. For example, at Norwich, which though much restored is well worth a visit, school parties are taken to the cells of an old prison. Deborah, aged eight, wrote, "The walls were damp and the place was as musty as a churchyard after rain. The guide shut the heavy door. It creaked and the sounds echoed down the passageway. Her footsteps died away and all the lights went out. It was like being trapped in a cave without air, light or space to move. Somebody near me rattled a chain. I wanted to scream. Then the lights came on and we were led up to the fresh air. I took a great breath of it and felt sorry for all the prisoners who had been shut up in such a grim hole".

Imaginative writing will also flow from events which children associate with castles — tournaments, feasts, soldiers on watch along the parapet walks, a visit of the king, a sortie into the enemy's encampment, can inspire even the least verbally gifted child. If these sorts of activity are attempted make sure source pictures are available (weapons, clothing, furnishing etc.). An ever increasing number of slide sets are now becoming available which also serve to illustrate mediaeval life. Some sets have been made from cinema stills, and provided one points out that not all the characters in English History looked like Peter O'Toole these strips have considerable value!

English literature provides another source. *Kenilworth* by Sir Walter Scott gives an over-romantic, anachronistic picture of castle life, but used with care it can do much to make history pictures come alive. Extracts may also be selected from:–

Anon   Sir Gawain; The Song of
                        Roland

*Dungeon is derived from "the safe place with a
 castle"– a donjon.

Chaucer	The knight's prologue
Arthur Conan Doyle	White Company; Sir Nigel
Keats	La belle dame sans merci
Anya Seton	Katherine
Spenser	Faerie Queene
Shakespeare	The historical plays
Tennyson	Lady of Shalott
J. Tolkien	Lord of the Rings (Part 3. Chapter X)
T. H. White	Sword in the Stone

The age of knight and castle was rich in colour and pattern, and this will also inspire model and picture-making. Shield designs worked on stiff card* (with brass push-through paper clips for rivets) invariably appeal to boys, long flowing paper banners to girls. As before, encourage the use of source books so that designs are based upon traditional practice. Collage knights and their ladies (made in paper or fabric) are another possibility. Here all manner of braids, ric-rac, sequins, metallic papers, foil, velvet, fur, may be incorporated into the picture. A firm mounting board is essential for work of this type as well as a reliable adhesive (Marvin or a similar acrylic based binder). It is worth remembering that fine details can be added to collage pictures with either acrylic paint or with Finart wax crayons (both of which may be applied successfully to fabric, paper or card).

Castle models may be as complicated or as simple as one wishes. If earthworks (be they pre-Roman or post-Hastings) are being built, papier mâché is the cheapest and most satisfactory material. Newclay (see Appendix) which has the advantage over most other modelling materials of drying without cracks and crazes, should be used if accuracy is an important element in the final model. If the wooden ramparts are to be erected on the earthworks they should be mounted whilst the base is still soft.

The square Norman stone keep is particularly easy to model. A packing box is all that is required, corner towers being added from card (or smaller boxes). Cover the whole model with paste and paper scraps before painting. Use a mixture of soap flakes and powder paint* to colour the model. As the paint dries the soap powder bubbles will "pop", a painter's way of achieving stone walls. Doorways and windows should be added when the paint has dried. These are best cut from coloured paper as most children find it terribly difficult to paint in fine detail.

Plans of the castle could also be made. These might be simple mathematical drawings or take the form of "dimensional" maps. Children's books often contain end papers drawn in this style, plans and elevations being liberally mixed.

The map/plan could be extended by including some of the surrounding countryside. If this is done we come full circle — for the castle was built where it was for a reason, and involvement in plan-making may well help the least perceptive to grasp the fact.

*Mix two tablespoonsful of soap powder, one tablespoonful of black powder colour and two tablespoonsful of white powder colour in a water jar. Add water to form a thick cream (e.g. dropping consistency of batter).

*A prepared template should be used. The aim, after all, is to achieve a satisfactory design.

Stone Keep
(Dover Castle)

GLOSSARY

Allure
A wall walk along a curtain wall

Ashlar
Dressed and cut stone

Bailey
The courtyard

Barbican
Gateway

Bastion
Corner fortification

Corbels
Stone bracket for supporting a projecting battlement

Crenellations
Battlements on top of wall

Curtain
The wall enclosing the courtyard of the castle

Donjon
The keep

Embrasure
Open spaces in a crenellation through which archer shoots

Loophole
A slit in a wall for ventilation or for shooting through

Louver
An opening in the hall roof to let out smoke from a central fire.

Machicolation
Spaces (holes) left between corbels to enable the defenders to throw missiles downwards upon the attackers below

Merlons
The solid portions of a crenellation

Meurtrière
A murder hole (usually found in an entrance passage)

Motte
The earthen mound of an early castle

Portcullis
An iron or wood grating which could be dropped to block an entrance passage

Postern
Side gate

Putlogs
Beams which supported a projecting timber gallery. Putlog holes are often found just below the crenellations on the keep

Ward
The courtyard enclosure of a castle

UNIT 10

Along the coast

The sea has played a rather special part in our development as a nation. All round our coasts we can see evidence of man's struggle to master the sea, to use it for defence, for trade, for food and for pleasure. The growth (or decline) of our ports and harbours reflect the changing needs of industry or the Lords of the Admiralty. Ports like Ipswich, Great Yarmouth, Lydd, Romney and Dunwich (now no more than a small hamlet on a crumbling Suffolk cliff face) expanded in response to an ever-growing woollen industry and slowly died as steel, coal and cotton ushered in a revolution in our economy*

Dependence on the sea had a number of side effects – ships had to be built and serviced and the coastline defended in time of war (evidence of this stretches from the Roman forts on the Saxon shore, Henry VIII's great coastal forts, the nineteenth-century Martello Towers to the concrete gun emplacements of the 1940's). In addition to this services were established to aid sailors – lighthouses and lightships to warn them against natural hazards, coastguards to advise them on weather and shipping movements, and lifeboats (and latterly helicopters) to give help should they need it.

Increasing trade with the New World also had its effect. Liverpool and Bristol are far better placed for Atlantic traffic than the East Coast ports whose prosperity largely depended upon links with Europe.

Thus ships and the sailors who man them offer a number of starting points for work with children, and it would be possible to develop the study in some of the following ways:–

(1) **A Port** In Unit 3 I suggested that the history of the town be studied, its growth plotted and related to changes in the national economy. In this connection we should not forget the importance of the shipbuilding yards upon which some communities came to depend. Bucklers Hard in Hampshire, the shipyards at Deptford and Chatham could cope with wooden ships, but were ill equipped to meet the demands of iron, steel and steam. Children living near a port could look for evidence of shipbuilding (or ship repair) – it might be nothing more than a sign painted on the waterfront, a long disused dry dock or illustrations of the "last launching" culled from the files of the provincial newspaper (thus while the launching of the Great Eastern is commemorated by a plaque on the Thames waterfront, the fact that over 100 ships were built on the beach at Nairn (Caernarvonshire) between 1760 and 1880 will only be discovered by reference to contemporary records and prints). Alternatively the town might have a number of ships chandlers still doing business, there might be rope, tackle and sail-makers' workshops to visit, a slipway, dry dock and locks to draw and yards full of the hulls of small yachts or great tankers. In this

connection children of secondary age could well study the implications of living in a community whose very existence depends upon a particular heavy industry. The social history of the 1920's provides evidence enough of the dangers.

Ports are interesting places for children to visit, but it is vital to make arrangements well in advance (a letter to the Port Superintendent invariably results in useful literature being made available as well as relevant local addresses). Some port authorities will allow organised parties on to the quayside while others prefer school groups to see the port from a launch.

If the port is a large one, it might also prove worthwhile to invite a member of the police force who has responsibility for the riverfront to talk to the children about his work.

(2) **Boats** There are a number of maritime museums which could be visited – and several historic ships which can be explored (the Victory at Portsmouth, the Cutty Sark and Gipsy Moth at Greenwich and the Discovery at the Embankment, London).

A more positive link is for the school to affiliate with the Ship Adoption Society (H.Q.S. Wellington, Temple Stairs, Victoria Embankment W.C.2.). This gives the opportunity for a continuous dialogue between a particular ship and the school as well as making geographical studies more meaningful.

(3) **Lighthouses, lightships and sea marks**
These are the responsibility of the "Corporation of Trinity House of Deptford Strond", London. Lighthouses, of course, have the task of warning and guiding sailors as to their position and course – an idea which goes back to pre-Christian times*. Lighthouses which are on land welcome visitors (during daylight hours but not if

*The Pharos of Alexandria, c 247 BC, was one of the wonders of the Ancient World.

visibility is so poor as to necessitate the sounding of fog signals). The lightchamber is usually quite small and as it is usually impossible to accommodate whole classes, the lighthouse is essentially a place suitable for a "group" visit.

The Eddystone Lighthouse

A study of lighthouses could embrace both arts and sciences. They are comparatively easy to draw, and models (Appendix 3) can be wired so that the lantern lights. Scientific terms will obviously need clarification. Can we measure light ? How ? What do we mean by candle power ? How does a lighthouse beam flash ? What part do the lens and the prism play in this ? What is a prism ? What is a lens ? Is the fog signal as effective as a light ?

Does sound travel as quickly as light ? If the light can be seen at night its light pattern could be recorded with the aid of a stop watch. These readings could be compared with other lighthouses and lightships in the area to show how each station has a "call" of its own.

Speaking personally I have little interest in signalling at sea, but I have known boys for whom this particular area of study has a strange (almost macabre) fascination. Buoys, storm cones and flags might sound an uninspiring topic for a special study – but material there is in plenty. There are buoys to mark channels and to mark wrecks (each type having its own shape and colour code) and buoys which have lights. There are cones and lights to tell of storms and flags which inform (as well as decorate !). Visually a study along these lines can be most attractive – for there is a wealth of material to record with drawings and diagrams. Models to support the study may take the form of a lightship (Appendix 3) or buoys made from such things as small cans and yoghourt cartons.

Wreck buoy   Lighted acetylene
                         gas buoy

Starboard hand   Port hand buoy
buoy

A Lightship

A Lifeboat

(4) **Lifeboats and rescue services** The lifeboat service is run by the Royal National Lifeboat Institution which was founded by Sir William Hillary, T. Wilson and G. Hibbert in 1824 (although public interest had been aroused as early as 1785 when the first insubmersible boat had been built under the encouragement of the Prince of Wales). Lifeboats are housed all round our coast and school groups are encouraged to visit them, and the "tour" is invariably fascinating. Apart from meeting a "real" sailor, the children have the opportunity to stand on deck, handle some of the equipment and even wear lifejackets. One nine-year-old after such an experience remarked that he now understood a verse which had been used in assembly "O God, your sea is so great and my boat is so small".

Lifeboats, because of their complex equipment, are not easy things to model – although ten- and eleven-year-olds are often successful when using balsa wood (quick drying cement, sandpaper, sharp knives and a supply of Elastoplast are absolutely essential if this is

attempted). The boat house and slipway, however, are easy to construct from old boxes and scrap card (Appendix 3).

The lifeboat service works in close co-operation with the coastguards. Although coastguard stations may not be as romantic as lighthouses and lifeboats, most coastguards are willing to give up their time to talk to children. As part of their work involves rescuing people who have got into difficulty along the coast through utter thoughtlessness, carelessness or bravado, I try to arrange for a visit to a coastguard station whenever I take children to the coast. Periodically "mock" rescues are made to test equipment and the skill of the local life saving corps, and if this can be written into the school journey programme it will become the highlight of the children's stay.

An Air Sea Rescue Service (run by the military) has been working in close co-operation with the civil authorities since the last war. Visits to air stations are sometimes possible but requests should be made well in advance by writing to the Commanding Officer.

(5) **Buildings** In some coastal towns there will be individual buildings which deserve study. Some of our older towns have an interesting Custom House or Harbour Master's Office (e.g. King's Lynn, Norfolk; Poole, Dorset; South Quay, Great Yarmouth, Norfolk). Other subjects for drawing include fishermen's cottages (which are still to be found in our prettier coastal villages) and the town houses of the prosperous eighteenth-century sea captains. (These are often to be found in the most unlikely places such as the back streets of Deptford and Rotherhithe in S.E. London).

Local inns might also be worth visiting (See Unit 5), particularly if they have a nautical flavour (e.g. the Bounty, Maryport, Cumberland the Jack Tar, Newcastle-upon-Tyne; the Royal Oak, Cartmel, Lancashire). Many inns (not all of which are on the coast) also have links with smugglers.

(6) **People** Another approach to the study is to try to look for local links with a famous sailor, shipbuilder or explorer. Statues and house plaques provide a starting point for initial enquiries – as do tombs in the local church (see Unit 7). It is far better, however, if the group can be taken to see an exhibition connected with the person they are studying. For example relics of Drake can be seen at the National Maritime Museum, of Nelson at Portsmouth, of Henry Adams, Nelson's shipbuilder, at Bucklers Hard, Hampshire, of Admiral Blake at Bridgwater, Somerset, while, if the sea is being looked at through the life of a painter, need one go further than the work of Turner (The Tate, the National Maritime Museum).

(7) **Museums** A number of museums feature ships and the sea (Appendix 1) and some of these have exhibitions which relate to specific occupations, e.g.

Peterhead, Aberdeenshire, Whaling and herring curing

Bridport, Dorset, Net making

Dartmouth, Devon, Early steam power

Birkenhead, Cheshire, Ship building

Exeter, Devon, Working boats

The particular manner in which the study develops will largely be determined by the children's interest in the topic and the amount of local colour which is available (herring fishermen's children are likely to be able to contribute more than those whose fathers work in a factory in Birmingham or a shoe shop in Nuneaton).

Yet of all the themes considered in this book, the sea has perhaps the widest appeal as well as providing all manner of material for display. Children's drawings, models and descriptions can be supported by copies of contemporary documents (Jonathan Cape's admirable "Jackdaws"), all manner of maps, notes on navigation aids, (including the compass and star charts), a globe, a timetable of local tides, as well as appropriate picture and reference books. Children will want to incorporate into the display objects found along the shore – rocks and pebbles, seaweed, shells, sand samples, floats from fishing nets, in fact flotsam and jetsam of all kinds. Often the shape of these finds is enough to encourage a child to create fanciful creatures of his own.

Additional source material (including addresses and information on ship societies, model clubs and collectors items) is contained in the monthly magazine *Sea Breezes,* published by The Journal of Commerce & Shipping Telegraph Ltd., 19, James Street, Liverpool.

UNIT 11

Museums, art galleries and stately homes

We are never far from a museum – and the fact that this is as true for a child living in a country village as for a child living in London or Glasgow, means that museums can play a very real part in young people's learning. Whether we take a school party to a national institution (like the British Museum) or to see a small local collection housed over the municipal library, the same general principles apply. These may be briefly summarised as follows:–

(a) What are we going to see ? It seems to me essential that the children be made aware of the sort of things they might be expected to find at the museum. This will involve preparation on the teacher's part – for children are unlikely to get much from visiting the excellent Roman collections at Cirencester or St. Albans, for example, if their current work has embraced the Thames Basin to the exclusion of all else. The more specialist the collections (e.g. the Geological Museum,

London; the Transport Museum at York; the Inland Waterways Museum at Stoke Bruerne, Northamptonshire) the greater will be the need for adequate preparation. The way in which we present the collection in this pre-visit discussion will, of course, vary with the interests and abilities and age groups of the children concerned. For six-year-olds going to the Science Museum for the first time it might, for example, be little more than looking at pictures of aircraft; seven-year-olds going to the Tudor Rooms at the Geffrye Museum, London, could hardly do better than watch a film strip illustrating social life in 1540; less able ten-year-olds, however, might better understand the Maiden Castle exhibits at Dorchester through a story which illustrates, quite incidentally, the campaign of the Emperor Vespasian.

(b) How are we going to work ? Here the very nature of children's learning bridges the age barrier. Children learn by looking and talking and handling, and it is a sad reflection on many learning situations that this last essential ingredient is lacking, even in those museums which otherwise operate an utterly praiseworthy schools service.

Obviously children will require writing material and a small board to lean on. The sight of children trying to sketch and take notes into a soft-backed note book fills me with pain. Surely the worst possible way of encouraging children to write is to make it virtually impossible for them to do! If pencils are being used for notes, duplicates are essential, not only because curators dislike sharpenings being dropped into their copy of a fourth-century Grecian Urn, but because at least one child will lose his en route. Fibre-tipped pens and ball-points have a definite advantage over most other writing materials in most respects — they do not require sharpening, clip securely into pockets and are excellent for sketch work. If large drawings are to be attempted these are best worked in wax crayon or oil pastel on sugar paper. Portable tape recorders make possible accurate on-the-spot verbal descriptions of interesting exhibits and also save much time if lengthy captions are to be used as source material for follow-up work on return to school. Cameras may also be taken into many of the smaller museums, but it is as well to obtain permission for their use.

Again it is difficult to be specific on the best way for the children to work in the museum. Personally I do not give the children I work with quiz sheets or worksheets for, in my opinion, these tend to encourage a superficial approach. I am sure that a child who has drawn a Chippendale chair accurately will have learned far more about the Georgians than he would have done by completing a questionnaire with the appropriate one-word answers. I believe that meaningful learning is far more likely to take place if individuals are encouraged to look at things which interest them (the quiz method tells children what to look for and, by omission, what to ignore).

If the group are allowed to touch exhibits, writing can stem from the experience; indeed some museums even have handling trays so that this particular approach is actively encouraged.

Written work can also take the form of illustrated guide books, straightforward accounts or to be linked to the life and times of a particular person. Thus although a child might be studying the life of John Wesley after visiting his house (in Old Street, London, E.C.1), much additional social comment could be obtained from going to Hogarth House, Chiswick, or the Coram Foundation in Bloomsbury. I have also found that most children like making "museum" collections. For example, one child could make notes and drawings on earthenware pots, another on decoration and pattern on weapons and armour, a third on hair styles and hats, a fourth on lighting and so on.

(c) How long should we stay? Little is achieved if children view museums as places in which they march round crocodile fashion, slowly becoming more and more tired, gazing at case upon case of irrelevant exhibits. It is important that each visit should fire the child's imagination, deepen his understanding and provide the stimulus for further work in school. Over-stimulation, however, by giving the children far too much material for them to assimilate, is equally shortsighted. It is possible to see so much that one ends up by remembering nothing.

(d) How large should the group be? Is it possible by using teachers based at the museum, students in training (or parents who themselves are experts in particular subjects) to keep the groups to a reasonable size?

Now all the points raised in the preceding paragraphs assume that the teacher has had opportunity to visit the museum in advance but, particularly if the visit is being made as part of a school journey programme, this is not always possible. It is in such cases that the curator (or schools' officer) can be of tremendous use. The type of help forthcoming will obviously depend upon the facilities which the museum has at its disposal. There might be a children's lecture room (complete with a range of visual aids as at Newport, Monmouthshire) or a studio (as at Geffrye Museum, London). The curator might have local sites worth visiting (as at Dumfries) — or be in touch with local people, experts in their own fields, who are prepared to talk to school parties. At the very least a catalogue can be obtained which will indicate relevant subject areas and the hours of admission.

The services which a museum provides are rarely advertised, and pre-visit contact between teacher and curator is surely something of a necessity.

The past twenty years have seen many developments in the display techniques employed by museums. Open museums in which children (quite literally) can walk into a bygone age are of particular interest. At York, for example, it is possible to stroll down a 19th-century street, gaze into shop fronts and wander into the forecourt of an inn to examine a stage coach. At St. Fagans, Cardiff, there are furnished cottages illustrating the slowly changing social and economic conditions in the Principality since the Middle Ages. On a smaller, but no less impressive, scale are the several Shakespearean properties at Stratford, or Washington's house or The Open Museum of the North East which is slowly being established on Teesside and will extend realism still further to embrace working machinery and trams, factories, farms and trains.

Stately homes are, from a teaching point of view, nothing more than rather a special sort of museum. Their only drawback is that their contents tend to illustrate one aspect of life — the sophistications of a landed aristocracy. It seems to me important that children who

are wondering at the grace of living in an Adam mansion should also be reminded that for many the 18th-century was an age of poverty and degradation*.

The great houses of England are so plentiful that it would be pointless to try to list them here or to comment at length on the way their contents could be used. However, the following approaches might be attempted.

(a) The story of the house through the lives of the people who have lived in it, or who visited it (this is the successful recipe adopted by the writers of many son et lumière programmes).

(b) An alphabet of interesting contents (a simple guide).

(c) The architecture of specific areas within the building so that comparisons may be made (1) with other great period houses (2) with homes today.

Obvious examples here are bedrooms, kitchens, staircases and hallways.

(d) Through the work of architects concerned in its construction. (This invariably leads to an investigation of changing architectural fashion).

(e) Through the life and work of artists and craftsmen whose work is on display. This will include painters and sculptors, cabinet and tapestry makers, silver and goldsmiths, wood carvers and pargeters.

Before visiting a "stately home" it is important to write to make a reservation for the party. Some are in the care of the Ministry of the Environment and free admission for school parties is possible (provided application is made at least 14 days in advance).

*"Drunk for $\frac{1}{2}d$, dead drunk for a 1d, straw free".

Others are the responsibility of the National Trust, local and national museums (e.g. Ham House is administered by the Victoria & Albert) and, of course, of the descendants of the original owners. In this connection the catalogue *Museums and Galleries in Great Britain & Ireland* is an invaluable teachers' aid for it contains details of opening times, admission charges and addresses of most of our great houses (Index Publishers, Oldhill, London Road, Dunstable, Beds.) The catalogue is reprinted annually.

Mention has already been made of the importance of drawing children's attention to the work of artists and sculptors. Thus art galleries should notbe forgotten when planning children's visits. Portraits of local worthies might not appeal overmuch to us but they do provide plenty of material for discussion on the ever-changing world of fashion.

If there is a gallery near school which contains pictures painted by the great masters I would suggest that the children should at least be made aware of their existence during the time they spend at their Primary School.

Giving people the opportunity to appreciate – even at a rudimentary level – something of the inner eye of the great artist is surely an opening that we, as teachers, should never ignore.

UNIT 12

Industrial archaeology

It is perhaps a reflection on the age we live in that having dismantled and destroyed many of the more significant examples of the technology which made possible the tremendous changes wrought by the Industrial Revolution, we have had to found countless conservation societies to preserve and restore those which do remain. Thus dotted about the country are groups whose interests include the conservation of such things as early mill machinery, railway lines, steam ships, canal barges, gypsy caravans and traction engines.

An interest in the industrial past might not seem as rich in appeal to young children as castles and hill forts. However, I believe that if the history of the area is closely linked with the lives of the great entrepreneurs (like the Duke of Bridgewater, Edward Pease of Darlington or Benjamin Gott of Leeds) we should make some attempt to show that industrialists (as well as kings and politicians) have had tremendous influence on the development of the community.

The whole subject of industrial archaeology is so complex as to make generalised appraisal here of little value. However, the following lines of development might be considered.

(a) **Harnessing water** The development of the canals from 1760–1850 was as dramatic as that of the railways. Indeed by 1850 the whole of central England was linked by navigable waterways* and this necessitated the construction of numerous bridges, locks, tunnels and aqueducts. If there is a canal near school it deserves study but it would be wise to preface each canal walk with general remarks on water safety.

The tremendous variety of architecture along the canal bank means that there should be sufficient to interest the majority of children in the group. The bridges, in particular, deserve study. In addition to conventional foot and road bridges† (usually beautifully proportioned stone structures) swing bridges are quite common near docks and harbours. "Drawbridges" may also be found on some lengths of canal (e.g. the Oxford Canal). On these bridges a section is raised for canal traffic by means of a counterbalance. In addition to sketching and model making, canal bridges are worth examining very closely for visual "clues". Is there a commemorative plaque on the bridge to indicate when it was built or the name of the architect ? If the bridge is built of stone or brick is there a protective band on the corner

---

*(North of a line drawn from Bristol to London; South of a line drawn from Manchester to York.)

†See also Unit 4 on roads.

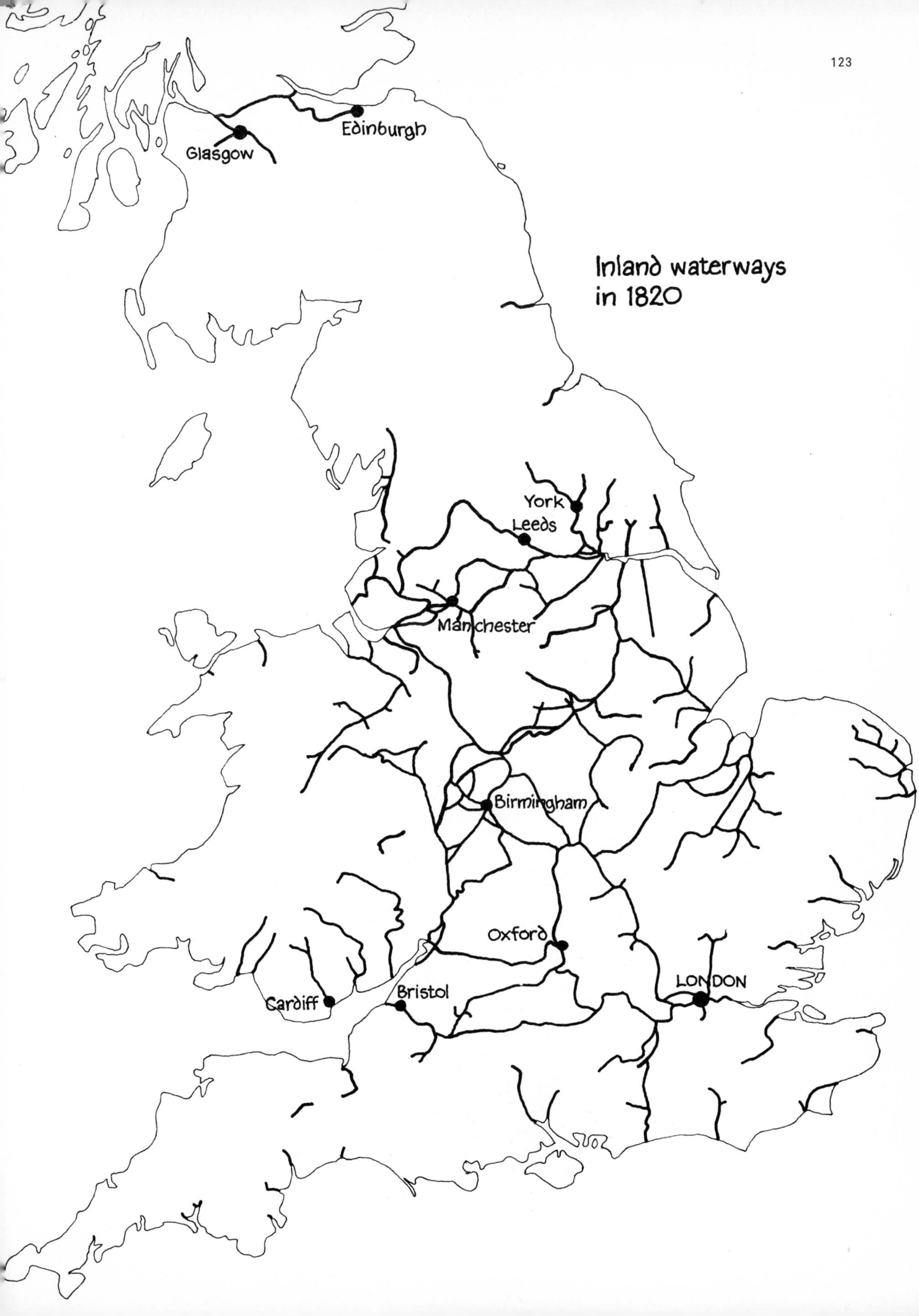

Inland waterways in 1820

Edinburgh

Glasgow

York
Leeds

Manchester

Birmingham

Oxford

Cardiff

Bristol

LONDON

of the soffit on the towpath side to prevent the towrope from wearing away the stone facing ? If the bridge is of iron is the name of the manufacturer still visible or the name of the works in which the metal was smelted ?

Aqueducts are less common than bridges but many are still in existence. Pontcysyllte, for example, which now carries pleasure craft to Llangollen (121 ft over the River Dee) was once part of the Ellesmere Canal. Some of the aqueducts were made of stone, others of metal.

In any event a study of the route of the canal or an Ordnance Survey map will indicate something of the physical problems which the canal builders had to overcome. Aqueducts were one method of controlling water levels – another was, of course, the lock.

Working locks are to be found on rivers and canals and the principle is sufficiently simple for even young children to grasp. A diagram to explain how a lock works can be modelled in synthetic clay (or Plasticine) and card

A Lock

Canal Barge

(Plate 36). Sometimes locks were built in "flights" – usually where it was necessary to raise the canal up the side of a valley. One of the most famous flights was on the Kennet & Avon canal near Devizes in Wiltshire which consisted of 29 "steps".

So much for the bank – what of the traffic which the canal carries ? If the canal is still in use, maps and diagrams could be made to show barge routes and the time which it takes to travel by water between neighbouring towns so that comparisons may be made in the road/rail communications. Canal barges are not difficult to model. The child who enjoys work with a fine brush will certainly enjoy decorating the boat's superstructure.

By the towpath, toll houses and pump houses might also be discovered though many nowadays are in such a sad state of repair as to be almost unrecognisable. The pump houses were required because the canal builders needed to ensure that an adequate reserve of water was always readily available. When a canal crossed a hillside water sometimes had to be pumped from below if no natural high level source was available.

Tolls for the use of the canal were charged on mileage Iron "mile posts" can still be found on many towpaths. Indeed we are fortunate that iron was *the* material of the canal age –

all manner of interesting inscriptions and sign posts remain and many well worth recording with rubbings (see Page 29).

If the children have made a study of inns near school, they would find it worthwhile to make note of "canal side" inns and their signboards. These often reflect the canal age, rejoicing in such titles as The Jolly Bargeman, The Towpath, The Barge and The Navigation. In the heyday of the canals these inns would also have had stables for the boatman's horse and the observant child might well be able to discover where these were situated.

Canal development (like that of the railways a century later*) had a considerable influence on the growth of towns. Thus in the forty years between 1801 and 1841, the population of

*See Unit 13.

Cast iron mile-post

Birmingham increased by 112,000, that of Leeds by 99,000 and that of Manchester by 180,000. Even towns which could hardly be considered pacemakers on the industrial front showed considerable population increases over the same period – Cambridge by 14,000, Bath by 20,000, York by 12,000, Reading by 9,000, Oxford by 14,000*. Apart from Birmingham, whose first navigable waterway dates from 1772, all of the towns mentioned had had some form of inland navigation since 1760.

Older children – especially if they have been fortunate enough to have spent a school journey touring on a canal barge – would benefit from visiting the Inland Waterways Museum (Stoke Bruerne, Northamptonshire) which contains everything from decorated barges, watercans, pumps and pictures to mementoes of the gangs who did the digging.

While on the subject of water, it is also worth finding out whether there are any water mills near school which might be worth a visit. They are picturesque buildings to draw, simple to model (Plate 35) and give children some understanding of a source of power rarely used to-day. Children of secondary age who are lucky enough to have a teacher whose Maths and Science are as sound as his model-making, might like to attempt Smeaton's experiment on water wheels. The earliest wheels (5000 of them were recorded in Domesday) were mainly of the undershot variety, i.e. the water drove against the bottom of the wheel. Later wheels (14th century onwards) were overshot, i.e. the water drove against the top of the wheel. Smeaton discovered that the overshot wheel gave over 40 per cent more power for the same waterflow and wheel size.

*The figures here are based on B. R. Mitchell's Abstract of British Historical Statistics published in 1962.

(b) **Harnessing the wind** Windmills are not as common now as they were at the time of Richard Cobbett who noted in *Rural Rides* that he counted seventeen as he approached Ipswich. However, they are still comparatively plentiful (particularly in the south east of England) and so deserve some comment here.

There are, broadly speaking, two kinds of windmill. The post mill, oldest type of windmill, is so called because its wooden frame was supported by a massive upright post which enabled it to be turned bodily into the wind. Chaucer's Miller would certainly have worked in one of these for it is the post mill that we find pictured in contemporary carvings (e.g. Bristol Cathedral). An improvement in mill design occurred in the late fourteenth century when a moveable top section was built onto a fixed frame. This meant that only the sails needed to be turned to face the wind. The earliest mills of this type were called "smock" mills and were built of wood. ("Smock" mills because they resemble in silhouette a'man in a smock.)

The basic idea of the smock mill (i.e. a revolving cap) was quickly incorporated into stone and brick buildings known as tower mills. Children will enjoy visiting a mill, particularly if it is in working order. Having visited Saxted Green (Suffolk) with a group of children I have a number of lady colleagues who will testify that the climb to the loft was the most nerve-racking experience they have had since they began teaching!

As a subject for picture-making the English mill has perhaps attracted more than its fair share of attention from landscape artists. However, there is no reason why children should not be encouraged to sketch in crayon or oil pastel. Remember, however, that not every child need draw the whole mill. By encouraging children to concentrate on particular aspects of the mill a much better understanding of its form and structure will be obtained and this will be particularly

Smock Mill,
Cranbrook, Kent

Bourn Post Mill, Cambridge

place to look in, for small animals were often used to turn the spit. A treadmill still in working order, which was used for raising water, may be seen at Carisbrooke Castle (Isle of Wight).

(d) Harnessing Steam The first steam engine to be put to industrial use was Thomas Slavery's "fire engine". It was designed to pump water from the tin and copper mines of the West country and patented in 1698. Thomas Newcomen's "atmospheric engines" which appeared in 1712 were used extensively in coal, tin, lead and iron mines and were an improvement on Slavery's design, but it took the combined skill of Watt, Boulton, Smeaton and Trevithick to perfect the beam engine.

Children who live in mining areas will find plentiful evidence of the old engine sheds (e.g. Streatham, Cambridgeshire; Nant y Mwyn Carmarthen; Glyn Pit, Glamorgan; Boscaswell Tin Mine, Cornwall) and though many are gaunt and rather forbidding they are well worth exploring with a small group. Beam engines are to be seen in many industrial museums. If children are particularly interested in gaining better understanding of how the machine works they could hardly do better than make a model from one of the Airfix plastic kits (available from most good toy shops).

The Museum of the North East has acquired a number of interesting engines and these will be seen working when the museum eventually opens. Engines on view will include the Beamish winding engine and the Wardle low haulage engine (which was originally designed by George Stephenson in 1823).

Tower Mill, Woodbridge, Suffolk

valuable for follow-up work at school. Thus some children could draw the sails, the cap or the fantail from various viewpoints while the rest of the group make simple silhouette drawings to show the overall shape of the mill.

Finally it is well to note that not all mills were used for grinding corn. Some (particularly in low-lying areas) were used solely for drainage purposes.

(c) Harnessing animals
Treadmills
Fortunately these machines are very much a thing of the past. Yet we can still find evidence of their use. Kitchens are probably the best

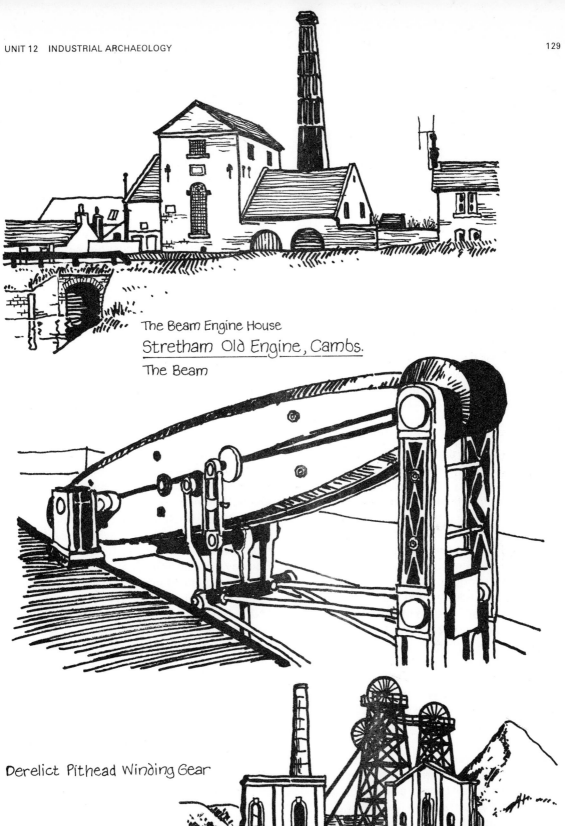

The Beam Engine House
Stretham Old Engine, Cambs.
The Beam

Derelict Pithead Winding Gear

UNIT 13
Railways

So much has been written on the "Age of Steam" that there seems little point in my dealing with the topic in great detail in this volume.

However, it is necessary to remind children that communications are absolutely essential to economic development and every civilisation has had to evolve its own system. Adequate communications not only facilitate the passage of goods and the movement of people, but, more important, the spread of ideas.

When studying the area around school, the local railway is often one of the oldest pieces of industrial development available. The railways, the growth of which mushroomed after the successful completion of the Liverpool and Manchester line (1826–1830) by George and Robert Stephenson, are still with us. The tracks follow the lines laid down by the early pioneers, their bridges, viaducts and cuttings a continual reminder of the skill of the Victorian engineer. Even in this age of railway closure the evidence remains.

Thus, while it is important that children should be aware how railways developed piecemeal, with numerous small companies establishing local lines, our starting point can be much more immediate.

Look at an Ordnance Survey map of the locality. Where does the railway run? Is its path straight, does it cling to a ridge or bend gently to take advantage of a river valley? Did the geology of the area have to be taken into account? The files of local newspapers

might throw some light on apparently odd twists and turns that cannot otherwise be understood. The construction of railways was not always popular with landowners who were not always prepared to accept compensation for the soot, smoke and dirt of the early engine.

Following the railway on a map naturally leads to following it on foot. On this walk (particularly if it be in a country area) the children should look for evidence of the early pioneers. These are often to be found on the ironwork of bridges and on the metal notices which abound on any length of track (particularly near stations, level crossings and signal boxes). Many of these signs were erected before the passing of the 1921 Railway Act. This act created the London Midland and Scottish Railway; The London North Eastern Railway; The Great Western Railway; and the Southern Railway, by amalgamating 120 small companies*. Thus in addition to notices placed by the LMS, LNER, GWR and SR, many signs still bear the names or initials of their original operators – The London and South Western Railway; the London and North Western; the London Chatham and Dover; the Southampton and Dorchester Railway; the Lancaster and Preston Railway; the Newcastle and North Shields Railway; the Greenwich and Blackwall Railway. Where the notices are not too near the track (e.g. on stations, by pedestrian crossings or country lanes), rubbings could be taken with crayon on detail paper (see Page 29). The walk should take in the local

*These four companies were themselves amalgamated to form British Rail after World War II.

station – but to visit it, it is necessary to first obtain permission from the Divisional Manager of the Region (the stationmaster will have his address).

Railways, of course, had a tremendous effect upon England. Whole new areas were opened up, towns appeared where none had existed before. Swindon, Eastleigh and Crewe owe as much to the Cheap Trains Act of 1844 as more romantic places owe to long dead City Fathers. Barrow-in-Furness had 250 people before the railway came (1841). In 1881 over 47,000 were living there.

Local studies might suggest answers to such questions as:– Where does the railway line go to ? What important towns are on its route ? How long ago was the line established ? A current timetable will prove of use in this connection, as well as providing much material for mathematics.

Model-making based on a railway theme allows for a variety of work from detailed engines assembled from commercially produced kits to less accurate (though more educationally valid) models made from junk and card (Appendix 3). Railway architecture is another possible development – models being made on a scale which would allow for their incorporation in toy track layouts.

The study may be extended through visits to the transport museums – at Clapham (London S.W.4) ; the Science Museum (which boasts the original Rocket), Swindon and York. It is well to remember that non-specialist museums often have transport sections. For example William Hedley's "Wylam Dilly" (1814) may be seen at the Royal Scottish Museum, Edinburgh.

Railway preservation societies also encourage party bookings, perhaps because the organisers are themselves rather eccentric enthusiasts ! In any event a ride by a steam engine is something of an event. Finally one

can try taking the sounds of the railway into the classroom. Argo have a long list of sound portraits in steam, though for me Honegger's tone poem "Pacific 321" evokes the living power of a great locomotive rather better than the rattle of the real thing.

Bibliography for Railway Studies
Catalogue of Railway Literature, David & Charles Ltd., Newton Abbot, Devon.

British Railway History (Vol 1, 2) by Hamilton Ellis, published by Allen & Unwin.

Regional History Series, David & Charles Ltd., Newton Abbot, Devon.

APPENDIX 1

A county by county gazetteer

Author's note

This section is meant only to serve as an indication of some of the riches of our countryside. It has proved most difficult to classify some of the buildings . . . some stately homes are castles which are also museums . . . and some of our cathedrals have private museums of their own which would deserve a visit even if the cathedral were closed (e.g. Durham). It has also proved impossible to include every church, every smock mill and every castle. Thus I would ask the reader to regard my list as a starting point – adding his own particular favourites, county by county, to mine. Our joint list should be most impressive!

BEDFORDSHIRE

Art Galleries & Museums

Bedford	Cecil Higgins Art Gallery *Water colours*
Luton	Museum & Art Gallery *Local history*

Buildings

Stevington	Postmill

Churches

Dunstable	St. Peter *1150 onwards*
Flitton	St. John the Baptist *15 C*
Leighton Buzzard	All Saints *13 C*
Luton	St. Mary *13–15 C*
Marston Mortaine	St. Mary *c 1450*
Shillington	All Saints *c 1300*
Wymington	St. Laurence *14 C paintings, brasses*

Homes & Palaces

Luton	Luton Hoo *dates from 1767 much restored c 1840s*
Woburn	Woburn Abbey *built c 1740*

BERKSHIRE

Art galleries & museums

Newbury	Borough Museum *local*
Reading	Museum & Art gallery *local*
Reading	Museum of English Rural Life *folk*
Windsor	Guildhall Museum *local*

Bridges & roads

Abingdon	Abingdon Bridge *dates from 1416*

Buildings

Great Coxwell	Tithe Barn *c 1250*

Castles
Windsor   Windsor Castle

Churches
Aldworth   St. Mary   *14 C*

Education
Eton   Eton College
                   parts of Henry VI's building
                   still survive

Pre-Christian
Nr. Ashbury   Alfred's Castle

Nr. Ashbury   Uffingham Castle
                   hill fort

Lambourn   Seven Barrows
                   a group of over 20 barrows

Pitstone   Postmill

Ibstone   Smock Mill

Churches
Bledlow   Holy Trinity
                   12 C with mediaeval wall
                   paintings

Chicheley   St. Laurence   *14 C*

Gayhurst   St. Peter   *18 C*

Quainton   Holy Cross
                   17 C, 18 C monuments

Stewkley   St. Michael
                   Norman carvings

Wing   All Saints
                   Norman remains
                   incorporated into 13 C
                   building

BUCKINGHAMSHIRE

Art galleries & museums
Aylesbury   County Museum
                   archaeology and history

High Wycombe   Museum & Exhibition
                   Rooms   *furniture making*

Old Warden   The Shuttleworth Collection
Aerodrome   *aviation, cars, carriages*

Waddesdon   Museum of Small Arms
                   Waddesdon Manor

Buildings
 Industrial
Brill   Postmill

CAMBRIDGESHIRE

Art galleries & museums
Cambridge   Fitzwilliam Museum
                   paintings, library,
                   illuminated manuscripts

Bridges & roads
Nr. Newmarket   Devil's Ditch
                   prehistoric trackway

Buildings
 Administrative
Cambridge   The Cambridge Colleges

Domestic	
Ely	Bishop's House *13 C hall*
Cambridge	Magdalene Street *Mediaeval houses and cottages*
Chippenham	Model village *built 1800*
Industrial	
Bourn	Postmill
Great Chishill	Postmill
Madingley	Postmill
West Wratting	Smock Mill
Inns	
Benet Street	Eagle Inn

Churches

Cambridge	Holy Sepulchre *Norman round church*
Cambridge	King's College Chapel *15 C*
Ely	Cathedral
Isleham	St. Andrew *14 C Hammerbeam roof*
March	St. Wendreda *double hammerbeam roof*
Trumpington	St. Mary & St. Michael *14 C with brasses*

Homes & palaces

Wisbech	Peckover House *built 1722*

CHESHIRE

Art galleries & museums

Altrincham	*local history*
Birkenhead	Williamson Art Gallery & Museum *water colours, ceramics, ship building*
Port Sunlight	Lady Lever Art Gallery *English furniture*
Stockport	Municipal Museum *local*

Buildings

Administrative	
Chester	The Mediaeval Wall
Chester	The Rows
Domestic	
Nantwich	Almshouses *date from 1640*

Churches

Astbury	St. Mary *14 C*
Great Brickworth	St. Mary & All Saints *14 C*
Nantwich	St. Mary *14 C*

Homes & palaces

Congleton	Little Moreton Hall *moated 16 C hall*
Gawsworth	Gawsworth Hall *Elizabethan Manor*

Knutsford	Tatton Park *Georgian Mansion*		

CORNWALL

Abbeys & priories
Tintagel	*foundations of Celtic monastery*

Art galleries & museums
East Looe	Cornish Museum *local history & craft*
Harlyn Bay	Harlyn Bay Museum *local Iron Age finds*
Helston	Borough Museum *local*
Tresco, Isle of Scilly	Valhalla Maritime Museum
Penzance	Natural History Museum *local*
St. Ives	Folk Museum
Truro	County Museum *local*

Bridges & roads
Saltash	Royal Albert Bridge *completed in 1859 by I. K. Brunel*
Camelford	Slaughter Bridge *(possible site of Arthur's last battle with Mordred)*
Wadebridge	*c 1470*

Castles
Nr. Falmouth	Pendennis Castle
St. Mawes	St. Mawes Castle
Tintagel	Tintagel Castle

Churches
Altarnun	St. Nonna *16 C bench ends*
Blisland	St. Protus & St. Hyacinth *12 C wagon roof*
Morwenstow	St. Morwenna *c 1150*
St. Germans	St. Germanus *12 C*

Homes & palaces
Nr. Bude	Penfound Manor *dates from Saxon times*
Nr. Torpoint	Anthony House *Georgian*

Pre-Christian
Between St. Ives & Penzance	Chysauster *Iron Age village*
Nr. St. Neot	The Hurlers *stone circles*

COUNTY DURHAM

Abbeys & priories

| Durham | Monkwearmouth Abbey |
| | *dates from c 670* |

Art galleries & museums

Durham	The Bowes Museum, Barnard Castle *Art collection*
Durham	Roman Fort Museum *Roman*
Durham	Gulbenkian Museum of Oriental Art
South Shields	The Museum *Maritime*

Bridges & roads

Barnard Castle	Stone Bridge *14 C ?*
Tanfield	Causley Arch Railway Bridge *1727*
Elvet Framwellgate Prebends }	The Wear Bridges

Castles

Barnard Castle	Barnard Castle
Durham	Durham Castle
Staindrop	Raby Castle

Churches

Escomb	St. John the Evangelist *Saxon*
Hartlepool	St. Hilda *13 C*
Pittington	St. Lawrence *c 1170*
Seaham	St. Mary *13 C*
Sedgefield	St. Edmund *Brasses & effigies*
Staindrop	St. Mary *13 C onwards* *many effigies*

Homes & palaces

| Washington | Washington Old Hall *Jacobean Manor House* |

CUMBERLAND

Abbeys & priories

| Nr. Brampton | Lanercost Priory *12 C* |

Buildings

| | Hadrian's Wall *Roman Wall* |

Castles

| Ravenglass | Muncaster Castle |
| Wetheral | Castle Corby |

Churches

| Great Salkeld | St. Cuthbert *c 1200* |

DERBYSHIRE

Art galleries & museums
Crich   Crich Tramway Museum

Derby   Museum & Art Gallery
                     local history

Cromford   Cromford Bridge   *15 C*

Buildings
Industrial
Cromford   Old Mill
                     an early Arkwright factory

Churches
Ashbourne   St. Oswald
                     13 C with 200 ft spire

Ashover   All Saints
                     interesting monuments

Bakewell   All Saints
                     *12 C, many interesting
                     monuments*

Repton   St. Wystan   *Saxon crypt*

Sandiacre   St. Giles   *12 C*

Homes & palaces
Chatsworth   Chatsworth House

Nr. Chesterfield   Hardwick Hall   *Tudor*

Nr. Derby   Kedleston Hall
                     Georgian mansion

Melbourne   Melbourne Hall
                     dates mainly from early 1700

Pre-Christian
Nr. Monyash   Arbor Low
                     *henge monument
                     barrow & bank*

Nr. Edale   Mam Tor
                     Iron Age hill fort

DEVON

Abbeys & priories
Buckfast   Buckfast Abbey
                     completed 1938

Art galleries & museums
Dartmouth   Borough Museum
                     nautical

Plymouth   City Museum
                     variety of collections

Torquay   Torquay Natural History
                     Museum   *local*

Bridges & roads
Barnstaple   Long Bridge
                     dates from 1273

Bideford   Bideford Bridge   *c 1450*

Sydenham   Horsebridge   *c 1440*
Darmeral

Buildings
Administrative
Exeter   Guildhall
                     dates from 1466

Exeter   Town walls

Tiverton   Blundells Old School
                     c 1600

Domestic
Nr. Totnes   Dartington Hall
                        Great Hall built c 1400

Inns
Barnstaple   The 3 Tuns tavern
                        15 C hostelry

Lighthouses
Ilfracombe   Mediaeval
                        Chapel-Lighthouse

Plymouth   Eddystone Lighthouse
                        18 C, re-erected on
                        Plymouth Hoe

Castles
Nr. Exeter   Powderham Castle

Totnes   Berry Pomeroy Castle

Churches
Atherington   St. Mary   *15 C*

Harberton   St. Andrew
                        14 C with wagon roof

Hartland   St. Nectan
                        14 C with wagon roof

Honeychurch   St. James
                        Norman with wagon roofs

Tiverton   St. Peter   *15 C*

Homes & palaces
Nr. Plymouth   Saltram House
                        Tudor House, re-styled 1740

Pre-Christian
Nr. Seaton   Blackberry Castle   *Hillfort*

Nr. Yelverton   Trowlesworthy Warren
                        Bronze Age moorland
                        settlement

DORSET

Abbeys & priories
Sherborne   Sherborne Abbey

Art galleries & museums
Bridport   Bridport Museum
                   local history

Dorchester   County Museum
                   local history

Poole   Old Poole House   *local*

Poole   Poole Museum   *local*

Shaftesbury   Abbey Ruins Museum
                   local
                   Local history Museum

Buildings
   Administrative
Blandford Forum   Town Hall

Wareham   Town walls

   Industrial
Swanage   Millpond

   Lighthouse
Portland   Old Lighthouse   *1869*

Castles
Corfe Castle   Corfe Castle

Churches

Affpuddle	St. Laurence	*13 C*
Bere Regis	St. John the Baptist	*12 C, superb wooden painted roof*
Blandford Forum	St. Peter & St. Paul	*Georgian*
Cerne Abbas	St. Mary	*15 C*
Hilton	All Saints	*15 C*
Whitchurch Canonicorum	St. Candida	*12 C*
Wimborne	St. Cuthberga	*12 C chained library*
Worth Matravers	St. Nicholas	*12 C*

Homes & Palaces

Athelhampton	Athelhampton Hall	*Tudor mansion*

Pre-Christian

Cerne Abbas	Cerne Abbas Giant	*Romano-British hill figure*
Nr. Dorchester	Maumbury Rings	*Stone circle*
	Maiden Castle	*Hill fort*
Nr. Nettleton	Eggardon	*Hill fort*
Nr. Wimborne	Badbury Rings	*Hill fort*

ESSEX

Abbeys & priories

Maldon	Beeleigh Abbey	*founded 1180*
Nr. Maldon	St. Osyth's Priory	*13 C*
Waltham	Waltham Abbey	*founded 1030*

Art galleries & museums

Barking	Valence House Museum	*local history*
Colchester	Colchester & Essex Museum	*local history*
Southend-on-Sea	Prittlewell Priory Museum	*local*

Buildings
Administrative

Nr. Colchester	Gatehouse – Layer Marney Towers	
Finchingfield	Guildhall	*c 1500*
Thaxted	Guildhall	*dates from 1475*

Domestic

Great Coggeshall	"Paycocke's" Merchants House	*c 1500*

Industrial

Cressing	Cressing Temple Barley Barn – Wheat Barn *date from c 1450*
Colchester	Water Mill *built c 1600*
Terling	Smock Mill

Inn

| Dedham | Sun Hotel *16 C* |

Castles

| Colchester | Colchester Castle |
| Castle Hedingham | |

Churches

Arkesden	St. Mary *13 C*
Bradwell-on-Sea	Church of St. Peter on the Wall *Saxon, dating from c 660*
Hadstock	St. Botolph *Saxon*
Little Maplestead	St. John the Baptist *14 C Hospitaller church*
North End	Black Chapel *Timber framed church*
Greensted, Ongar	St. Andrew *Saxon*
Saffron Walden	St. Mary *15 C*

Homes & palaces

| Audley End | Audley End *Jacobean/Georgian Mansion* |
| Nr. Halstead | Gosfield Hall *Tudor Courtyard House* |

GLOUCESTERSHIRE

Abbeys & priories

| Tewkesbury | Tewkesbury Abbey *c 1150* |

Art galleries & museums

Blaise Hamlet	Blaise Castle House *folk*
Bristol	City Art Gallery & Museum *British & European Art*
Chedworth	Chedworth Villa *Roman Museum*
Cirencester	Corinium Museum *Roman relics*
Gloucester	Folk Museum

Bridges & roads

| Bristol | Clifton Suspension Bridge *I. K. Brunel 1830* |

Buildings

Industrial

| Arlington | Arlington Mill *Flour Mill 17 C* |
| Ashleworth | Tithe Barn |

Castles
Berkeley   Berkeley Castle

St. Briavels   Milo Fitzwalter

Churches
Bishops Cleeve   St. Michael   *12 C*

Bristol   St. Mary Redcliffe   *13 C*

Chipping   St. James   *15 C*
Campden

Cirencester   St. John the Baptist
                      14-15 C wool church

Deerhurst   St. Mary
                      *Saxon with mediaeval
                      additions*

Eastleach   St. Martin & St. Michael
                      Norman

Fairford   St. Mary   *15 C, fine glass*

Kempsford   St. Mary   *15 C*

Leonard Stanley   St. Leonard   *12 C*

Newland   All Saints   *13 C*

Northleach   St. Peter & St. Paul   *15 C*

Quenington   St. Swithin
                      Norman carving

Winchcombe   St. Peter   *15 C wool church*

Homes & palaces
Badminton   Badminton House
                      Georgian

Nr. Bath   Dyrham Park
                      dates from c 1690

Chipping Sodbury Doddington House
                      Regency

Nr. Gloucester   Elmore Court
                      Tudor with late addition

Horton   Horton Court
                      12 C Norman Hall

Uley   Owlpen Manor
                      *Cotswold stone manor
                      dating from 15 C*

Winchcombe   Sudeley Castle
                      dates from c 1450

Pre-Christian
Great Witcombe   Roman Villa

HAMPSHIRE

Abbeys & priories
Christchurch   Christchurch Priory   *c 1150*

Netley   Netley Abbey

Romsey   Romsey Abbey
                      founded 907

Art galleries & museums
Alton   Curtis Museum
                      folk & natural history

Basingstoke   Wallis Museum
                      *coins, medals, clocks,
                      watchmakers' tools*

Beaulieu	The Motor Museum – Montague House
Bucklers Hard	Maritime Museum
Christchurch	Red House Museum *local history*
Isle of Wight	Museum of Geology
Arreton (Isle of Wight)	Arreton Manor *Toys, furniture, folk*
Silchester	Calleva Museum *Roman*
Southampton	Bargate Guildhall *local*
	God's House Tower *local*
Southampton	Wool House *Maritime*
Southsea	Southsea Castle Museum *Military & Naval*
Southsea	Cumberland House Museum
Winchester	City Museum *local*
Winchester	Westgate Museum *local civic*

Buildings
Administrative
| Southampton | Mediaeval fortifications |

Commemorative
| Nr. Winchester | Rufus Stone |

Domestic
| Isle of Wight | Brading Villa *Roman* |

Industrial
Bembridge (Isle of Wight)	Bembridge Windmill *dates from 1700*
Wickham	Water Mill *c 1815*
Southampton	Wool House *14 C merchant*

Lighthouse
| Isle of Wight | St. Catherine's Point – Lighthouse *c 1320* |

Castles
Odiham	Odiham Castle
Porchester	Porchester Castle
Winchester	Castle Hall

Churches
| Arreton (Isle of Wight) | St. George *12 C* |
| Avington | St. Mary *18 C box pews* |

Homes & palaces
| Isle of Wight | Osborne House *home of Queen Victoria* |

HEREFORDSHIRE

Art galleries & museums
| Hereford | City Museum & Art Gallery *local* |
| Hereford | Churchill Gardens Museum *costume, dolls* |

Bridges & roads
| Nr. Ross-on-Wye | Wilton Bridge *1597* |

Buildings
Domestic
| Ross-on-Wye | Almshouses – Church Street *c 1600* |

Castles

Croft   Croft Castle

Goodrich   Goodrich Castle

Churches

Garway   St. Michael   *12 C*

Hoarwithy   St. Catherine   *19 C*

Holme Lacy   St. Cuthbert   *14 C*

Kilpeck   St. Mary & St. David
               Norman

Ledbury   · St. Michael   *13 C*

Moccas   St. Michael   *c 1150*

Tyberton   St. Mary   *18 C*

Homes & palaces

Much Marcle   Hellens
               *Manor House, occupied
               since 1292*

Nr. Pontrilas Kentchurch Court
               14 C fortified Border house

Pre-Christian

Aconbury   Aconbury Camp
               Iron Age fort

HERTFORDSHIRE

Art galleries & museums

Ashwell   Ashwell Village Museum
               *life of English village
               from prehistory to
               modern times*

Hertford   The Museum   *local*

St. Albans   Roman Museum

Buildings

Administrative

St. Albans   Clock Tower
               completed 1412

Domestic

Rickmansworth Piccotts End
               14 C hall house

Entertainment

St. Albans   Roman Theatre

Industrial

St. Albans   Silk mill   *18 C*

Inns

St. Albans   Fighting Cocks Inn
               mediaeval inn

Ware   Bull Inn   *dates from 16 C*

Castles

Hertford   Hertford Castle

Churches

Aldbury   St. John the Baptist   *13 C*

Broxbourne   St. Augustine   *15 C*

Sawbridgeworth   St. Mary   *14 C*

St. Albans   St. Michael   *Saxon*

Homes & palaces

Hatfield   Hatfield House   *Jacobean*

Knebworth   Knebworth House
                 *Tudor, with Victorian
                 Gothic overtones*

HUNTINGDONSHIRE

Abbeys & priories

Ramsey   Ramsey Abbey
                 *church of St. Thomas a
                 Becket*

Thorney   Thorney Abbey
                 *old foundation, much
                 ravaged*

Art galleries & museums

Peterborough   Museum & Art Gallery
                 local

Bridges & roads

Huntingdon   Huntingdon Bridge
                 c 1300

Wansford   The Bridge   *c 1580*

Buildings
Inns

Stilton   The Bell Inn
                 18 C coaching inn

Churches

Barham   St. Giles   *12-13 C*

Peterborough   Cathedral

Homes & palaces

Stamford   Burghley House
                 Elizabethan

KENT

Abbeys & priories

Canterbury   St. Augustine's Abbey
                 c 1150

Art galleries & museums

Canterbury   Beaney Institute
                 local history

Dartford   Borough Museum
                 local history

Tunbridge Wells Museum & Art Gallery
                 local

Bridges & roads

Maidstone   East Farleigh Bridge   *14 C*

Buildings
Domestic

Nr. Sevenoaks   Old Soar Manor
                 Knights House c 1200

Industrial

Biddenden	The Cloth Hall *dates from mediaeval times*
Cranbrook	Smock Mill

Lighthouses

Dover	Roman Lighthouse – Dover Castle
Margate	Lighthouse

Castles

Deal	Deal Castle
Dover	Dover Castle
Hever	Hever Castle
Lamberhurst	Scotney Castle
Lympne	Lympne Castle
Maidstone	Allington Castle
Rochester	Rochester Castle
Walmer	Walmer Castle

Churches

Barfreston	St. Nicholas *12 C*
Canterbury	St. Pancras *Saxon*
Dover	St. Mary in Castro – Dover Castle *Saxon, much restored*
Hever	St. Peter *14 C with brasses*
Hythe	St. Leonard *13 C*
Maidstone	All Saints *14 C*
Sandwich	St. Clement *14 C*
Stone	St. Mary *13 C*

Homes & palaces

Nr. Cranbrook	Sissinghurst Castle *Tudor mansion, fortified house*
Eynsford	Lullingstone *Tudor, largely re-built during 18 C*
Sevenoaks	Knole House *Tudor*
Nr. Sevenoaks	Ightham Mote *14 C moated manor*
Tunbridge Wells	Penshurst Place *dates from 1340*
Westerham	Squerryes Court *built c 1680*

Pre-Christian

Nr Aylesford	Kits Coty House *chambered barrows*
Nr Farningham	Lullingstone Villa *Roman Villa*
Richborough	The Roman Fort

LANCASHIRE

Abbeys & priories

Furness	Furness Abbey *c 1150*

Art galleries & museums

Bury	Art Gallery *British 19 C artists*
Didsbury, Manchester	Fletcher Moss Gallery *English water colours*
Eccles	Monks Hall Museum *local*
Lancaster	The City Museum *local*
Liverpool	City Museum *local*
Liverpool	Walker Art Gallery *European & British paintings*
Manchester	City Art Gallery *English Masters*
Manchester	Chethams Library *collection of books 16-18 C*
Manchester	Gallery of English Costume, Platt Hall
Manchester	Whitworth Art Gallery *Prints, drawings, textiles*
Northenden, Manchester	Wythenshawe Hall *local*
Ribchester	Museum of Roman Antiquities
Rossendale	Rawtenstall Museum *local*
Rufford	Old Hall & Folk Museum *folk*
Salford	Science Museum *mining*
St. Helens	Pilkington Museum of Glass *glass*

Bridges & roads

Nr. Littleborough	Blackstone Edge *Roman paved roadway over Pennines*

Buildings
Industrial

Manchester	Liverpool Road Station *oldest railway station in the world, 1830*
Lytham St. Annes	Tower Mill

Castles

Hornby	Hornby Castle
Lancaster	Lancaster Castle

Churches

Billinge	St. Aidan *18 C*
Cartmel	St. Mary the Virgin *15 C*
Halsall	St. Cuthbert *14 C*
Sefton	St. Helen *14 C brasses*

Homes & palaces

Nr Bolton	Turton Tower *Manor house dating from 12 C*
Chorley	Astley Hall *Jacobean*
Liverpool	Speke Hall *Tudor courtyard house*

LEICESTERSHIRE

Art galleries & museums

Leicester	Jewry Wall Museum *local history to 1500*
Leicester	Leicester City Museum *local*

Castles

Ashby de la Zouch

Churches

Appleby Magna	St. Michael	*14 C*
Ashby de la Zouch	St. Helen	*15 C*
Breedon on the Hill	St. Mary & St. Hardulph *Norman, with some carvings from c 800*	
Staunton Harold	Staunton Harold Church *a Cromwellian church*	

Homes & palaces

Belvoir	Belvoir Castle	*Regency*
Nr Loughborough	Prestwold Hall *18 C house*	
Melton Mowbray	Stapleford Park *dates from 1500*	

LINCOLNSHIRE

Abbeys & priories

Crowland	Crowland Abbey *founded 716*

Art galleries & museums

Gainsborough	Old Hall Museum	*folk*
Grimsby	Doughty Museum *ships and seamen*	
Lincoln	City & County Museum *local, emphasis on Roman Lincoln*	
Lincoln	Usher Art Gallery	*clocks*
Spalding	Ayscoughfee Hall *natural history*	

Bridges & roads

Lincoln	High Bridge	*16 C*
Crowland	Triangular Bridge	*14 C*

Buildings

Administrative

Lincoln	Roman Town Gate

Domestic

Stamford	All Saints Place
	Barn Hill, Broad Street
	groups of 17-18 C houses
Boston	Fydell House
Lincoln	The Jew's House
	Steep Hill *12 C house*
Bourne	South Street
	Tudor cottages

Inns

Stamford	George Hotel
	18 C coaching inn

Castles

Lincoln	Lincoln Castle
Tattershall	Tattershall Castle

Churches

Barton upon Humber	St. Peter *Saxon*
Boston	St. Botolph *14 C*
Grantham	St. Wulfram
	12 C onwards
Heckington	St. Andrew *15 C*
Horncastle	St. Mary *Many brasses*
Louth	St. James *16 C*
Sleaford	St. Denys *12 C*
Spalding	St. Mary & St. Nicholas
	13 C
Stow	St. Mary *Saxon – Norman*

Homes & Palaces

Belton Kesteven	Belton House
	attributed to Wren

Burgh le Marsh	Gunby Hall	*House 1700*
Nr Grantham	Woolsthorpe Manor	
	17 C house	
Nr Lincoln	Auburn Hall *16 C house*	

LONDON

Abbeys & priories

Charterhouse Square E.C.1.	The Charterhouse	*c 1370*
Westminster S.W.1	Westminster Abbey	
	3 C onwards	

Art galleries & museums

Museum Street W.C.1	The British Museum
Coram Fields W.C.1	Coram Foundation
	old masters
	Handel mementoes
Woburn Square W.C.1	Courtauld Institute
	Impressionist and
	post-impressionist
Hampstead Grove N.W.3	Fenton House
	early musical instruments
Kingsland Road E.2	Geffrye Museum
	period rooms
Exhibition Road S.W.7	Geological Museum
Basinghall Street E.C.1	Guildhall Museum *Roman*

London Road S.E.23	Horniman Museum *ethnography and musical instruments*
Kensington Palace W.8	London Museum *local*
Clapham High Street S.W.4	Museum of Transport
Greenwich S.E.10	National Maritime Museum
Cromwell Road S.W.7	Natural History Museum
Trafalgar Square W.C.2	National Gallery *European painting*
St. Martin's Lane W.C.2	National Portrait Gallery
Chancery Lane W.C.2	Public Records Office
Kew Gardens	Royal Botanic Museum *botany*
Buckingham Palace S.W.1	Royal Mews *state coaches, cars and harness*
South Kensington S.W.7	Science Museum
13 Lincolns Inn Fields W.C.2	Soane Museum *antiquities and paintings*
Millbank S.W.1	Tate Gallery *British paintings & modern art*
Tower of London E.C.3	Tower Armouries
Cromwell Road S.W.7	Victoria & Albert Museum

Manchester Square W.1.	Wallace Collection *arms & armour, paintings, French china & furniture*
Euston Road N.W.1	Wellcome Medical Museum

Bridges & roads

London S.E.16	Rotherhithe Tunnel *I. K. Brunel*
London E.1	Tower Bridge *opened 1894*
London S.E.1	Waterloo Bridge

Buildings
   Administrative

London S.W.1	Buckingham Palace
London E.C.2	Guildhall
Old Palace Yard S.W.1	Jewel Tower
London S.W.1	Palace of Westminster

   Entertainment

London S.E.1	Royal Festival Hall

   Industrial

Wimbledon Common S.W.19	Post Mill
London W.C.1	The G.P.O. Tower
London S.E.1	The Shell Building

   Inns

Borough High Street S.E.1	The George *coaching inn*

Castles

London E.C.1	Tower of London

Churches

Byward Street E.C.3	All Hallows by the Tower *Saxon onwards*

Smithfield E.C.1	St. Bartholomew the Great *Norman*
Paul's Wharf E.C.4	St. Benet *Wren*
Fleet Street E.C.4	St. Bride *Wren, rebuilt*
Strand W.C.2	St. Clement Danes *Chapel of the R.A.F.*
Bishopsgate E.C.2	St. Ethelburga *14 C*
Bishopsgate E.C.2	St. Helens *c 1200*
Tower of London E.C.1	St. John's Chapel *Norman*
Trafalgar Square W.1.	St. Martin in the Fields *c 1720*
Cheapside E.C.4	St. Mary le Bow
Euston Road N.W.1	St. Pancras *c 1820*
Walbrook E.C.4	St. Stephen Walbrook *Wren*
Tower of London E.C.1	St. Peter ad Vincula *c 1500*
St. James's Palace	Queen's Chapel *c 1620*
Inner Temple E.C.4	Temple Church *Norman*
Birdcage Walk	The Guards' Chapel

Homes & palaces

| Burlington Lane W.4 | Chiswick House *Palladian mansion* |

London W.8	Kensington Palace *dates from 1689*
Hampstead Heath N.W.3	Kenwood House *Georgian mansion*
Lambeth Palace Road S.E.1	Lambeth Palace *dates from 1230*
Pall Mall S.W.1	St. James's Palace *dates from 1530*

MIDDLESEX (Greater London)

Art galleries & museums

| Brentford | British Piano Museum |
| Enfield | Forty Hall *17-18 C, Art* |

Homes & palaces

Brentford	Syon House *Georgian mansion*
Hampton	Hampton Court Palace *dates from 1514*
Osterley	Osterley Park House *built 1761-1780, Adam decoration*
Twickenham	Strawberry Hill *Horace Walpole's "Gothick" house*

NORFOLK

Abbeys & priories

Binham	Binham Priory	*c 1200*
Castle Acre	Castle Acre Priory	*c 1100*
Nr Holm	St. Benets Abbey *founded c 810*	
Thetford	Thetford Priory	
Walsingham	Walsingham Priory	*12 C*
Little Walsingham	Shrine of Our Lady	*c 1150*

Art galleries & museums

Great Yarmouth	Maritime Museum for East Anglia
Norwich	St. Peter Hungate Museum *church art*
Norwich	Strangers Hall Museum
Thetford	Ancient House Museum *local*

Bridges & roads

Pedders Way	(runs from East coast across the county)

Buildings

Administrative

King's Lynn	Custom House *dates from c 1420*
King's Lynn	Guildhall
Norwich	Strangers Hall *14 C*
Thetford	Town gaol – Cage Lane *c 1580*

Domestic

Castle Rising	Alms Houses *Stuart*
Wells next the Sea	Buttland – round the green *18 C*
North Elmham	Cathedral & Manor House ruins *c 800*
Norwich	Tombland *Georgian square*

Industrial

Berney Arms	Drainage Mill
Great Yarmouth	The Quayside on the River Yare *group of riverside buildings*
Burnham Overy	Tower Mill

Inns

Thetford	Bell Hotel *built c 1500*
Scole	White Hart *coaching inn 18 c*

Castles

Caister on Sea	Caister Castle
Castle Rising	The Castle
Norwich	Norwich Castle

Churches

Acle	St. Edmund	*11 C onwards*
Elsing	St. Mary	*14 C*
North Runcton	All Saints	*18 C*
Norwich	St. Peter Mancroft	*c 1440*
Ranworth	St. Helen	*fine screen*

Sall	St. Peter & St. Paul	*15 C*
Swaffham	St. Peter & St. Paul *15 C hammerbeam roof*	
Trunch	St. Botolph *15 C hammerbeam roof*	
Wymondham	St. Mary & St. Thomas *dates from c 1110*	

Homes & palaces
Nr Aylsham	Blickling Hall	*Jacobean*
Nr Swaffham	Oxburgh Hall *moated mediaeval mansion*	
Wells	Holkam Hall *Palladian mansion built 1734-59*	

Pre-Christian
Nr Brandon	Grimes Graves *Neolithic mine shafts*

NORTHAMPTONSHIRE

Art galleries & museums
Northampton	Central Museum *shoe making, local*
Northampton	Abingdon Park Museum *folk*

Churches
Barnack	St. John the Baptist	*Saxon*
Brixworth	All Saints	*dates from c 800*

Church Stowe	St. Peter & St. Paul *Saxon west tower*	
Earls Barton	All Saints *Saxon – Norman with mediaeval additions*	
Northampton	Holy Sepulchre	*c 1110*
Whiston	St. Mary	*16 C carvings*

Buildings
Commemorative crosses
Hardingstone	Eleanor Cross
Northampton	Eleanor Cross, London Road

Homes & palaces
Nr Corby	Deene Park	*Tudor*
Gretton	Kirby Hall *Tudor house (ruins)*	
Nr Kettering	Rockingham Castle *Tudor house*	
Nr Northampton	Althorp House	
Nr Northampton	Castle Ashby *Elizabethan with additions*	
Nr Northampton	Delapre Abbey	

Pre-Christian
Nr Adderbury	Rainsborough Camp *oval hill fort*

NORTHUMBERLAND

Abbeys & priories
Hexham	Hexham Abbey *c 1100*
Holy Island	Lindisfarne Priory *c 1200*

Art galleries & museums
Newcastle-upon-Tyne	Hancock Museum *Zoology, Botany*

Bridges & roads
Hexham	Haglut Burn Bridge
Newcastle-upon-Tyne	High Level Bridge *Robert Stephenson 1849*
Twizel Bridge	(longest span of a mediaeval bridge in England)

Buildings
Administrative
Berwick-on-Tweed	The City Wall *built 1565*
	Hadrian's Wall *Roman wall*
Hexham	Moot Hall *15 C*

Castles
Alnwick	Alnwick Castle
Warkworth	Warkworth Castle

Churches
Elsdon	St. Cuthbert *14 C*
Ovingham	St. Mary *13 C*

Homes & palaces
Nr Newcastle	Seaton Delaval Hall *1718–28*

NOTTINGHAMSHIRE

Abbeys & priories
Worksop	Priory of St. Cuthbert & St. Mary *founded c 1100*

Art galleries & museums
Nottingham	Nottingham Castle Museum *Lace. Local crafts*

Churches
Newark-on-Trent	St. Mary Magdalene *15 C*

OXFORDSHIRE

Abbeys & Priories
Dorchester	Dorchester Abbey *c 1100*

Art galleries & museums
Filkins	Filkins & Broughton Poggs Museum *folk*
Oxford	Ashmolean Museum *great masters, silver, musical instruments, coins*

Oxford	History of Science Museum *early astronomical, mathematical, optical instruments*
Oxford	University Museum *mainly zoology, entomology, geology*
Woodstock	Oxford County Museum *local*

Bridges & roads

Abingdon	Abingdon Bridge *1416*

Buildings
Administrative

Oxford	The Oxford Colleges

Domestic

Nr Woodstock	North Leigh Villa

Industrial

Mapledurham	Mapledurham House – Water Mill

Castles

Banbury	Broughton Castle

Churches

Bloxham	Our Lady *14 C*
Ewelme	St. Mary the Virgin *15 C (interesting misericords)*
Iffley	St. Mary *12 C*
Oxford	St. Mary the Virgin *15 C*
Stanton Harcourt	St. Michael *14 C* *monuments*
Witney	St. Mary *14 C*

Homes & palaces

Blenheim	Blenheim Palace *Queen Anne*

Enstone	Ditchley Park *Georgian*
Mapledurham	Mapledurham House *Tudor manor house*

SHROPSHIRE

Abbeys & priories

Nr Cressage	Buildwas Abbey *c 1150*
Nr Ditherington	Haughmond Abbey *c 1300*
Nr Donnington	Lilleshall Abbey *c 1150*
Much Wenlock	Wenlock Prior *c 1185*
Shrewsbury	Shrewsbury Abbey *founded 1080*

Art galleries & museums

Coalbrookdale	Museum of Ironfounding
Munslow Aston	The White House *folk*
Shrewsbury	Rowley House Museum *Roman*

Bridges & roads

Iron Bridge	Iron Bridge *built by Abraham Darby 1777–9*

Buildings
Administrative

Bridgnorth	Town Hall *c 1650*

Castles

Ludlow	Ludlow Castle

Churches

Adderley	St. Peter *Gothic Revival 1801*
Bridgnorth	St. Mary Magdalene *designed by Thomas Telford the engineer*
Claverley	All Saints *mediaeval wall painting*
Longnor	St. Mary *13 C*
Ludlow	St. Laurence *c 1300*
Madeley	St. Michael *designed by Thomas Telford*
Pitchford	St. Michael *c 1200*
Shifnal	St. Andrew *mainly 16 C*
Shrewsbury	St. Mary *14–16 C glass*
Tong	St. Bartholomew *15 C effigies*

Homes & palaces

Craven Arms	Stokesay Castle *12 C fortified manor*
Nr Ludlow	Whitton Court *house dating from c 1140*
Shifnal	Boscobel House *Jacobean hunting lodge*
Shrewsbury	Attingham Hall *Georgian mansion*

Pre-Christian

Nr Wroxeter	The Wrekin *hill fort*

SOMERSET

Abbeys & priories

Cleeve	Cleeve Abbey *c 1200*
Glastonbury	Glastonbury Abbey *12 C*
Nr Winsham	Forde Abbey *c 1150*

Art galleries & museums

Bath	Holbourne of Menstrie Museum *China, furniture, paintings*
Bath	Bath Assembly Rooms – Museum of Costume
Bath	Victoria Art Gallery
Glastonbury	Lake Village Museum *finds from Iron Age village*
Taunton	County Museum – The Castle *local*
Weston-super-Mare	Municipal Museum *local*
Yeovil	Borough Museum *local*

Buildings
Administrative

Glastonbury	The Abbey Courtroom *15 C*

Domestic

Bath	The Roman Baths
Glastonbury	The Abbey – Abbot's Kitchen *late 14 C*
Clevedon	The Manor House – Clevedon Court *14 C*
Bath	Royal Crescent

Castles

| Dunster | Dunster Castle |
| Nunnery | Nunnery Castle |

Churches

| Yatton | St. Mary *14 C* |

Homes & palaces

Greenham	Cothay Manor *dates from c 1300*
Somerton	Lytes Cary *14 C manor house and chapel*
Nr Yeovil	Montacute House *Tudor mansion*

Pre-Christian

Cheddar	Goughs Cave *Ice Age home*
Nr Cheddar	Wookey Hole Cave *caves occupied c 300 BC onwards*
Nr Sparkford	Cadbury Castle *hill fort*

STAFFORDSHIRE

Art Galleries & museums

Barlaston	Wedgwood Museum *pottery*
Blithfield	Museum of Childhood & Costume
Brierley Hill	Brierley Hill Museum *local & foreign glass*
Great Haywood	County Museum – Shugborough *local*
Tamworth	Castle Museum *local*
Wall	Roman Museum
Walsall	E. M. Flint Art Gallery *local*

Churches

Alrewas	All Saints *12 C*
Bilston	St. Leonard *Regency*
Eccleshall	Holy Trinity *12 C*
Gnosall	St. Laurence *12 C onwards*
Penkridge	St. Michael & All Angels *13 C*
Stafford	St. Chad *12 C*
Tamworth	St. Editha *14 C*
Tutbury	St. Mary *11 C*

Homes & palaces

| Nr Wolverhampton | Moseley Old Hall *Tudor mansion* |

Pre-Christian

| Cannock | Castle Ring *hill fort* |

SUFFOLK

Abbeys & priories

Bury St Edmunds	The Abbey	*c 1000*
Nr Bury St Edmunds	Ixworth Abbey	*12 C*

Art galleries & museums

Bury St Edmunds	Moyses Hall	*local history*
Ipswich	Ipswich Museum *local, particularly Saxon*	
Ipswich	Christchurch Mansion *period rooms*	

Buildings

Administrative

Butley	Gate House at Butley Priory *14 C*
Bury St Edmunds	Guildhall *15 C*
Lavenham	The Guildhall *c 1530*
Woodbridge	Shire Hall *c 1570*

Domestic

Bury St Edmunds	Mayses Hall *a Norman building*

Clare	Mediaeval Houses *dating from 1470*	
Lavenham	Church Street	*Tudor houses*

Industrial

Framsden	Post Mill	
Saxted Green	Post Mill	*c 1700*
Woodbridge	Tower Mill	
Nr East Bergholt	Flatford Mill – *Water Mill 18 C*	

Castles

Burgh Castle	Burgh Castle
Framlingham	Framlingham Castle
Orford	Orford Castle

Churches

Bacton	St. Mary *14 C (hammerbeam roof)*
Boxted	Holy Trinity *hammerbeam roof*
Eye	St. Peter & St. Paul *15 C*
Framlingham	St. Michael *15 C*
Fritton	St. Edmund *12 C*
Hessett	St. Ethelbert *15 C*
Lavenham	St. Peter & St. Paul *15 C (wool church)*
Long Melford	Holy Trinity *15 C*
Mildenham	St. Mary & St. Andrew *c 1300*
Stoke by Nayland	St. Mary *brasses*
Hawstead	All Saints *Norman with many brasses*

Homes & palaces

Nr Bury St.   Ickworth
Edmunds   *Palladian mansion*

Heveningham   Heveningham Hall
                   Palladian house built c 1779

Petworth   Petworth House
                   built 1688–96

Nr Sudbury   Melford Hall
                   Tudor mansion

Stoke d'Abernon   St. Mary   *13 C brasses*

Homes & palaces

Nr. Guildford   Albury Park   *Queen Anne*

Nr. Guildford   Clandon Park   *Georgian*

Nr. Lingfield   Puttenden Manor
                   dates from 1477

Nr. Richmond   Ham House
                   Jacobean house

Buildings
   Memorial
Kingston-upon-   Coronation Stone
Thames

SURREY

Art galleries & museums

Farnham   Willmer House Museum
                   local

Haslemere   Sir Jonathan Hutchinson's
                   Educational Museum
                   Geology & zoology

Weybridge   Museum   *local*

Castles

Farnham   Farnham Castle

Churches

Chaldon   St. Peter & St. Paul
                   *famous mediaeval wall
                   painting*

Lingfield   St. Peter & St. Paul
                   *15 C misericords,
                   chained bible*

SUSSEX

Abbeys & priories

Battle   Battle Abbey   *c 1200*

Nr. Hailsham   Michelham Priory
                   founded 1229

Art galleries & museums

Bignor   Bignor Museum
                   Roman remains

Bramber   Handicraft Museum –
                   St. Mary's

Brighton   Motor Museum

Brighton   Thomas-Stanford Museum
                   Preston Manor
                   silver & furniture

Chichester	City Museum *local history*
Chichester	Guildhall Museum *Roman relics*
Eastbourne	Towner Art Gallery *British artists 19 & 20 C*
Lewes	Anne of Cleves House *folk*
Shoreham	Marlipins Museum *local maritime*
Wilmington	The Museum *agriculture*
Worthing	Museum & Art Gallery *toys and dolls*

Buildings

Chichester	Market Cross
Chichester	Town Walls
Bignor	Roman Villa
Rye	Mermaid Street *buildings mainly 18 C but* *with much earlier work*

Castles

Arundel	Arundel Castle
Bodiam	Bodiam Castle
Hurstmonceux	Hurstmonceux Castle
Lewes	Lewes Castle
Pevensey	Pevensey Castle

Churches

Arlington	St. Pancras *Saxon. Norman remains*
Ashburnham	St. Peter *17 C*
Bosham	Holy Trinity *Saxon*

Etchingham	St. Mary & St. Nicholas *14 C*
New Shoreham	St. Mary de Haura *c 1150*
North Marden	St. Mary *c 1150*
Rye	St. Mary *12 C*
Shipley	St. Mary *Norman carving*
Sompting	St. Mary *Saxon tower*
Steyning	St. Andrew *12 C*
Trotton	St. George *14 C brasses*
Worth	St. Nicolas *Saxon*

Homes & palaces

Brighton	Royal Pavilion *Regency*
Chichester	Goodwood House *1780–1800*
Nr. Lewes	Firle Place *Georgian house*
Nr. North Marden (Nr. Petersfield)	Uppark *built 1690*
Nr. Chichester	Fishbourne *Roman villa*
Nr. Washington	Chanctonbury Ring *hill fort*
Wilmington	Long Man

WARWICKSHIRE

Art galleries & museums

Birmingham	City Museum *European painting, sculpture*
Birmingham	The Assay Office *silverware, coins, medals*
Birmingham	Museum of Science & Industry *machines, transport, gramophones, small arms*
Royal Leamington Spa	Art Gallery & Museum *20 C artists, ceramics, glass*
Warwick	County Museum *local*
Warwick	Doll Museum

Bridges & roads

Stratford-on-Avon	Clopton Bridge *c 1480*

Buildings

Alcester	Malt House *1500*
Birmingham	Yeoman's House — Blakesley Hall *16 C*

Castles

Nr. Coleshill	Maxstoke Castle
Kenilworth	Kenilworth Castle
Warwick	Warwick Castle

Churches

Astley	St. Mary *14 C*
Berkswell	St. John the Baptist *12 C*
Warwick	St. Mary *12 C onwards*

Homes & palaces

Alcester	Coughton Court *Elizabeth with Jacobean relics*
Alcester	Ragley Hall *built 1680*
Edgehill	Upton House *built c 1680*
Hockley Heath	Packwood House *Timber framed Tudor house*
Nuneaton	Arbury Hall *1750 onwards*
Nr. Stratford-on-Avon	Clopton House *Tudor & Jacobean*

WESTMORLAND

Buildings
Domestic
Kendal   Castle Dairy   *built c 1560*

Churches
Bolton   All Saints   *12 C*

Ormside   St. James   *c 1150*

Homes & palaces
Nr. Kendal   Levens Hall
                  Tudor mansion

Kendal   Sizergh Castle
                  dates from 14 C

WILTSHIRE

Art galleries & museums
Avebury   Alexander Keiller Museum
                  pre-history

Devizes   Museum   *local history*

Lacock   Agricultural Museum
                  tools & implements

Salisbury   Salisbury & South
                  Wiltshire Museum   *local*

Swindon   Great Western Railway
                  Museum

Buildings
Domestic
Melksham   Great Chalfield Manor
                  moated house c 1480

Bradford-on-   Orpin's House (Home of
Avon   Parish Clerk of Bradford)
                  built 1720

Memorial
Castle Combe   Market Cross   *15 C*

Churches
Amesbury   St. Mary & St. Mellor
                  12 C onwards

Bradford-on-   St. Laurence
Avon   *Saxon, dating from 7 & 8 C*

Cricklade   St. Sampson   *16 C*

Malmesbury   St. Mary   *12 C carvings*

Potterne   St. Mary   *13 C*

Homes & palaces
Chippenham   Corsham Court
                  Elizabethan

Nr. Hungerford   Littlecote
                  manor dating from 1490

Stourton   Stourhead
                  Palladian house

Nr. Warminster   Longleat House
                  dates from 1566

Wilton   Wilton House
                  dates from 1650

Pre-Christian
Avebury   Avebury Rings
                  *(see also Alexander Keiller
                  Museum)*

Nr. Amesbury   Normanton Down
                  barrow

Nr. Avebury	Overton Hill – The Sanctuary	
	Neolithic henge monument	
Nr. Marlborough	Silbury Hill	
	pre-roman mound	
Nr. Marlborough	West Kennet Barrow	
	Neolithic long barrow	
Nr. Salisbury	Old Sarum	
Nr. Salisbury	Stonehenge	
	Bronze Age Temple	
Nr. Salisbury	Woodhenge	
	Neolithic henge	
Nr. Stantonbury	Wansdyke	*earthworks*
Nr. Warminster	Battlesbury Hill	*hill forts*
Nr. Westbury	Bratton Castle	*hill fort*

Castles

Holt Heath	Holt Castle

Churches

Chaddesley Corbett	St. Cassian
	Norman with 14 C additions
Great Malvern	St. Michael & St. Mary
	15 C
Strensham	St. John *13 C*

Homes & palaces

Nr. Droitwich	Hanbury Hall
	red brick house c 1700
Kidderminster	Harvington Hall
	moated Tudor mansion
Nr. Kidderminster	Hartlebury Castle
	Palace of Bishops of Worcester built 1675

Pre-Christian

Nr. Eckingham	Bredon Hill *hill fort*

WORCESTERSHIRE

Abbeys & priories

Pershore	Pershore Abbey
	dates from Saxon times

Art galleries & museums

Dudley	Central Museum
	Geology (particularly coal)
Worcester	Dyson Perrins Museum
	ceramics

YORKSHIRE

Abbeys & priories

Nr. Ampleforth	Byland Abbey	*c 1130*
Beverley	Beverley Minster *Saxon onwards*	
Leeds	Kirkstall Abbey	*12 C*
Rievaulx	Rievaulx Abbey *founded 1131*	
Nr. Ripon	Fountains Abbey *founded 1132*	
Selby	Selby Abbey *11 C onwards (much restored)*	
Sheffield	Beauchief Abbey *founded 1175*	
Nr. Skipton	Bolton Priory	*c 1150*
Whitby	Whitby Abbey *refounded c 1070 on Saxon site*	
York	St. Mary's Abbey	*11 C*

Art galleries & museums

Batley	Art Gallery *contemporary artists*	
Bedale	Bedale Hall *domestic arts & crafts*	
Boroughbridge	Aldborough Roman Site Museum	
Bradford	City Art Gallery & Museum *paintings and local history of West Riding*	
Bridlington	Bayle Museum *weapons; domestic, trade and farm implements*	
Halifax	Shibden Hall	*folk*
Kingston-upon-Hull	Ferens Art Gallery *old masters, modern sculpture*	
Kingston-upon-Hull	Maritime Museum	
Leeds	Abbey House Museum *folk*	
Leeds	City Museum *geology & natural history*	
Leeds	City Art Gallery *old & modern masters*	
Middlesbrough	Dorman Memorial Museum *local*	
Rotherham	Municipal Museum	*local*
Scarborough	The Museum	*local*
Sheffield	City Museum	*cutlery*
York	Castle Museum	*folk*
York	Debtors Prison Museum *toys and costume*	
York	Railway Museum	

Bridges & roads

Wakefield	The Bridge *14 C with chapel*	

Buildings

Administrative

Nr. Scarborough	Roman signal station	
York	Guildhall	*built 1448 but largely restored*

York	Merchant Taylors Hall *14 C*

Domestic

York	The Shambles *Mediaeval Street*

Industrial

Sheffield	Abbeydale Industrial Village *18 C steelworks*

Castles

Conisbrough	Conisbrough Castle
Pickering	Pickering Castle
Pontefract	Pontefract Castle
Richmond	Richmond Castle
Scarborough	Scarborough Castle
Skipton	Skipton Castle
York	Cliffords Tower

Churches

Aldborough	St. Andrew *14 C*
Baldersby	St. James *Victorian*
Howden	St. Peter *14 C*
Kingston-upon-Hull	Holy Trinity *14 C*
Patrington	St. Patrick *14 C*
Ronaldkirk	St. Ronald *12 C*
Rotherham	All Saints *15 C*
Thirsk	St. Mary *c 1420*
Weaverthorpe	St. Andrew *12 C*
Whitby	St. Mary *18 C box pews*

Homes & palaces

Bradford	Bolling Hall *15 C onwards contains folk museum*
Bridlington	Burton Agnes Hall *Elizabethan*
Driffield	Sledmere House *Georgian mansion*
Keighley	East Riddlesden Hall *17 C manor house*
Nr. Leeds	Harewood House *country mansion built 1771*
Nr. Malton	Castle Howard *largely Queen Anne, dates from 1687*
Ripley	Ripley Castle *Early 14 C*
Ripon	Markenfield Hall *14 C moated manor*

SCOTLAND

Abbeys & priories

Angus	Arbroath	*founded 1178*
Nr. Alloa (Stirlingshire)	Cambuskenneth	*c 1300*
Nr. Melrose (Berwickshire)	Dryburgh Abbey	*c 1200*
Dunfermline (Fife)	Dunfermline Abbey	*c 1200*
Dunkeld (Perthshire)	Dunkeld Cathedral	*c 1400*
Elgin (Moray)	Elgin Cathedral	*c 1230*
Edinburgh (Midlothian)	Holyrood Abbey	*c 1200*
Iona (Argyle)	*founded c 1200, with 7 C traces*	
Jedburgh (Roxburgh)	Jedburgh Abbey	*12 C*
Kelso (Rox)	Kelso Abbey	*12 C*
Paisley (Renfrew)	Paisley Abbey	
Whithorn (Wigtown)	St. Ninians Priory	*12 C*
Kirkcudbright	Sweetheart Abbey *founded 1273*	

Art galleries & museums

Dumfries	The Observatory	*local*
Edinburgh (Midlothian)	John Knox House	*religious*
	Museum of Childhood	*toys*
	National Gallery of Modern Art	
	National Gallery of Scotland	
	National Museum of Antiquities of Scotland	
	Royal Scottish Museum	
Forfar (Angus)	Meffan Institute	*local*
Glamis (Angus)	Kirk Wynd	*folk*
Glasgow (Lanark)	City Art Gallery & Museum	
	Hunterian Museum *coins, Roman*	
	Museum of Transport *tram cars*	
Glenesk (Angus)	Museum	*folk*
Inverurie (Aberdeen)	The Museum	*local*
Kingussie (Inverness)	Highland Folk Museum	
Kirkcaldy (Fife)	The Museum	*local*
North Berwick (East Lothian)	Burgh Museum *natural history*	
Turriff (Aberdeen)	Delgate Castle	*armour*

Bridges & roads

Ayr (Ayrshire)	Auld Bridge	*13 C*
Bridge of Dun (Angus)	Bridge of Dun	*c 1780*
Aberfeldy (Perth)	General Wade's Bridge *1733*	

Dunkeld (Perth)	Dunkeld Bridge *built by Thomas Telford*
Dumfries	Dumfries Bridge *1290*
Queensferry (Nr. Edinburgh	Forth Railway Bridge *opened 1890 – contrast with New Bridge*
Berwick-upon-Tweed (N'umberland)	Royal Border Bridge *built by Robert Stevenson*
Craigellachie (Banffshire)	Spey Bridge *an iron bridge built by Thomas Telford in 1815*
Perth	Tay Bridge *1766*
Coldstream (Berwickshire)	Tweed Bridge (with Marriage House)

Buildings
Administrative

	The Antonine Wall (Dumbartonshire to Stirlingshire) *Roman wall built in c 140 AD, abandoned c 190 AD*

Domestic

Ousdale (Caithness)	Broch
Auldearn (Nairnshire)	Dove Cot *17 C*
Dirleton (East Lothian)	Dirleton Castle – Dove Cot *16 C*
Falkland (Fife)	Falkland Palace *hunting palace 16 C*
Anstruther (Fife)	The Manse *oldest inhabited manse in Scotland (1590)*

Nr. Lanark	New Lanark Model Village *established by Robert Owen in 1800*
Brechin (Angus)	Round Tower *c 110*
Edinburgh (Midlothian)	Stuart House – Gladstones Land

Industrial

Bonawe (Argyll)	Lord Furnace *a factory for smelting iron ore, built in 1753*
East Linton (East Lothian)	Preston Mill *18 C corn mill*

Religious

Stirling	Holyrood *15 C*
Roslin (Midlothian)	Roslin Chapel

Castles

Aberdour (Fife)	Aberdour Castle
Monikie (Angus)	Affleck Castle
Nr. Achranich (Argyll)	Ardtornish Castle
Balmoral (Aberdeen)	Balmoral Castle *(gardens only)*
Nr. Blair Atholl (Perthshire)	Blair Castle
Nr. North Middleton (Midlothian)	Borthwick Castle
Nr. Bankend (Dumfries)	Caerlaverock Castle
Nr. Kintocher (Aberdeen)	Craigievar Castle

Edinburgh (Midlothian)	Craigmillar Castle
Crichton (Midlothian)	Crichton Castle
Doune (Perthshire)	Doune Castle
Nr. Peterculter (Aberdeen)	Drum Castle
Nr. Stonehaven (Kincardinshire)	Dunnottar Castle
Nr. Golspie (Sutherland)	Dunrobin Castle
Nr. Blanefield (Stirling)	Duntreath Castle
Edinburgh (Midlothian)	Edinburgh Castle
Glamis (Angus)	Glamis Castle
Guthrie (Angus)	Guthrie Castle
Nr. East Linton (East Lothian)	Hailes Castle
Hermitage (Roxburgh)	Hermitage Castle
Kildrummy (Aberdeen)	Kildrummy Castle
Nr. Alva (Clackmannan)	Menstrie Castle
Stirling	Stirling Castle

Homes & palaces

Nr. Banchory (Kincardineshire)	Crathes Castle *Scottish baronial hall dating from 1550*
Nr. Methlick (Aberdeen)	Haddo House *built in 1732 by W. Adam*
Inveraray (Argyll)	Inveraray Castle *18 C French style chateau*
Linlithgow (West Lothian)	Linlithgow Palace *Royal manor dating from 1424*
Nr. Gordon (Berwickshire)	Mellerstain *dates from 1660s*
Edinburgh (Midlothian)	Palace of Holyrood House *c 1500 restored 1671-9*
Nr. Perth	Scone Palace *built 1803*
Innerleithen (Peebleshire)	Traquair House *oldest inhabited house in Scotland*

Pre-Christian

Burnswark (Dumfermline)	Annandale *hill fort & Roman camp*
Abington (Lanark)	Arbory Hill *hill fort*
Ardifuir (Argyll)	*circular galleried dun*
Nr. Culloden Muir (Inverness)	Balnuarin of Clava *ring cairn*
Nr. Amisfield Town (Dunfermline)	Barrs Hill *hill fort*
Nr. Echt (Aberdeen)	Barmekin of Echt *hill fort*
Rousay (Orkney)	Blackhamar *cairn*
Nr. Bathgate (West Lothian)	Cairnpapple *henge & cairns*

Bowden (Roxburgh)	Eildon Hills	*hill fort*
Mainland (Orkney)	Maes Howe	*chambered cairn*
Cullerlie (Aberdeen)	*stone circles*	

WALES

Abbeys & Priories

Anglesey	Penmon Priory	*c 1150*
Nr. Bridgend (Glam.)	Ewenny Priory	*c 1200*
Llanthony (Mon.)	Llanthony Priory	*c 1100*
Tintern (Mon.)	Tintern Abbey *founded 1131*	
Usk (Mon.)	Priory Church	

Art galleries & museums

Aberystwyth (Cardiganshire)	National Library of Wales & University College Museum	
Bangor (Caernarvonshire)	Penrhyn Castle	*dolls*
Caernarvon (Caernarvonshire)	Segontium Museum *Roman*	
Cardiff (Glam.)	National Museum of Wales	
Cardiff (Glam.)	St. Fagans Castle	*folk*
Newport (Mon.)	Museum & Art Gallery *local*	
Tenby (Pembrokeshire)	The Museum	*local*
Towyn (Merioneth)	Railway Museum	

Bridges & roads

| Bangor (Caernarvonshire) | Britannia Railway Bridge *Robert Stevenson 1850* | |
| Conway (Caernarvonshire) | Conway Suspension Bridge | |

Devil's Bridge   Devil's Bridge over the
(Cardiganshire)   River Mynach
                      three bridges, the earliest
                      being 12 C

Llangollen   Llangollen Bridge   *14 C*
(Denb.)

Llanrwst)   Llanrwst Bridge
(Caernarvonshire) *dates from 1636*

Nr. Bangor   Menai Suspension Bridge
(Caernarvonshire) *Thomas Telford, opened*
                      1826

Monmouth (Mon)   Monnow Bridge   *late 13 C*

Denbigh (Denb.)   Pont Cysyllte Aqueduct
                      Thomas Telford, completed
                      1805

Pontypridd   Pontypridd Bridge
(Glam.)   *completed 1775*

Chepstow (Mon.)   Severn Road Bridge
                      opened 1966

Buildings
Administrative
Ruthin (Denb.)   The Court House
                      built in 1450

Monmouth   Shire Hall   *c 1720*

Domestic
Nr. Llangoed   Penmon Priory
(Anglesey)   *dovecot & hermits cell*

St. Mary Church   Beaupre
(Glam.)   *Elizabethan manor ruins*

Conway   Plas Mawr
(Caernarvonshire) *Elizabethan town house*

Industrial
Nr. Pontypool   Glyn Pits
(Mon.)   *early pumping engines*

Religious
Clynnog Fawr   St. Beuno   *15 C*
(Caernarvonshire)

Holywell   St. Winifred's Chapel   *15 C*
(Flints.)

Wrexham (Denb.) St. Giles

Castles
Beaumaris   Beaumaris Castle
(Anglesey)

Caerphilly   Caerphilly Castle
(Glam.)

Caernarvon   Caernarvon Castle

Cardiff (Glam.)   Cardiff Castle

Chepstow (Mon.) The Castle

Chirk (Denb.)   The Castle

Nr. Brigend   Coity Castle
(Glam.)

Conway   Conway Castle
(Caernarvonshire)

Denbigh   Denbigh Castle

Ewloe (Flint.)   Ewloe Castle

Flint   Flint Castle

Harlech   Harlech Castle
(Merioneth)

Kidwelly   Kidwelly Castle
(Caernarvonshire)

Nr. Tenby   Manorbier Castle
(Pembrokeshire)

Nr. Hay-on-Wye   Painscastle
(Radn.)

Pembroke   Pembroke Castle

Raglan (Mon.)   Raglan Castle

Rhuddlan   Rhuddlan Castle
(Flint.)

Nr. Llangollen   Sycharth Castle
(Denb.)

Homes & palaces
Welshpool   Powis Castle
(Montgomery)   *13 C castle, restored c 1670*

Crickhowell   Tretower Court
(Brecon)   *fortified mediaeval house*

Pre-Christian
Reynoldston   Arthur's Stone
(Glam.)   *megalithic chamber*

Clynnog Fawr   Bachwen
(Caernarvonshire) *megalithic burial chamber*

Nr. Brecon   Brecon Gaer   *hill fort*

Nr. Llanddaniel   Bryn Celli Ddu   *cairn*
(Anglesey)

Nr. Moelfre   Din Lligwy
(Anglesey)   *Romano-British village*

Paviland (Glam.)   Goats Hole Cave
                       Palaeolithic burial place

APPENDIX 2

People and their homes

Jane Austen
J. A. House, Chawton, Hants

Sir James Barrie
Barrie's Birthplace, Kirriemuir, Angus

Admiral Blake
The A. B. Museum, Bridgwater, Somerset

Anne, Charlotte, Emily Brontë
The Parsonage, Haworth, Yorks

John Bunyan
Meeting House, Bedford, Bedfordshire

Robert Burns
Burns Cottage, Alloway, Ayrshire
Lady Stair's House, Edinburgh
Souter Johnnie's Cottage, Kirkoswald, Ayrshire

Lord Byron
Newstead Abbey, Nr. Kirkby in Ashfield, Notts

Thomas Carlyle
Carlyle House, Cheyne Row, London S.W.3
Carlyle's House, Ecclefechan, Dumfries

Lewis Carroll
(Charles Dodgson) Museum, Guildford, Surrey

Winston Churchill
Chartwell, Kent

Grace Darling
Church of St. Aidan, Bamburgh,
Northumberland

Charles Darwin
Downe House, Downe, Kent

Charles Dickens
Rochester Museum, Rochester, Kent
Dickens House, Doughty Street, London W.C.1
Commercial Road, Portsmouth, Hants
Bleak House, Broadstairs, Kent

Benjamin Disraeli
Hughenden Manor, High Wycombe, Bucks

Sir Francis Drake
Buckland Abbey, Devon

Edward Elgar
Elgar's Birthplace, Broadheath, Worcs

George Eliot
Museum & Art Gallery, Nuneaton,
Warwickshire

Thomas Gainsborough
Gainsborough House, Sudbury, Suffolk

Thomas Hardy
The County Museum, Dorchester, Dorset
Hardy's Cottage, Higher Beckhampton, Dorset

William Hazlitt
Chillington Manor, Maidstone, Kent

Sir Henry Irving
Russell-Cotes Museum, Bournemouth, Hants

Samuel Johnson
Johnson's Birthplace, Lichfield, Staffs
17 Gough Square, London

Rudyard Kipling
Batemans, Burwash, Sussex

John Milton
Milton Cottage, Chalfont St. Giles, Bucks

William Morris
W. M. Gallery, Forest Road, London E.17

Horatio Nelson
The Victory, Portsmouth, Hants
Nelson Museum, Monmouth, Mons

Florence Nightingale
Claydon House, Claydon, Bucks
Royal Army Medical Corps Museum, Aldershot,
Hants

Robert Owen
Memorial Museum, Newtown, Mont

Beatrix Potter
Hill Top, Nr. Sawrey, Lancs

Cecil Rhodes
Bishop's Stortford, Herts

Sir John Ross
Wigtown County Museum, Stranraer,
Wigtownshire

John Ruskin
Brantwood, Coniston, Westmorland
Ruskin Galleries, Bembridge, Isle of Wight
J.R. Museum, Coniston, Westmoreland

Capt. R. F. Scott
The Discovery, The Embankment,
London S.W.1

Sir Walter Scott
Abbotsford House, Nr. Galashiels,
Roxburghshire

Lord Shaftesbury
St. Giles House, Wimborne St. Giles, Dorset

William Shakespeare
The Shakespeare properties at Stratford-on-
Avon, Warks

George Bernard Shaw
GBS House, Ayot St. Lawrence, Herts

Edmund Spenser
Edmund Spenser's House, Alton, Hants

Alfred, Lord Tennyson
Farringford, Isle of Wight
Usher Art Gallery, Lincoln, Lincs

George Washington
Sulgrave Manor, Nr. Banbury, Oxon

James Watt
McLean Museum, Greenock, Renfrewshire
Kinneil House, Borrowstounness, West Lothian

Josiah Wedgwood
Wedgwood Museum Trust, Darlaston, Staffs

Duke of Wellington
Apsley House, Hyde Park Corner,
London S.W.1

John Wesley
Wesley's House, City Road, E.C.1

William Wilberforce
Wilberforce House, Kingston-upon-Hull,
Yorks

General James Wolfe
Quebec House, Westerham, Kent

William Wordsworth
Wordsworth House, Cockermouth,
Cumberland
Dove Cottage, Grasmere, Westmorland

APPENDIX 3

Working drawings (craft ideas)

Figures carved from polystyrene, using a knife or electric cutting tool. Decoration is added by dressing the figure with leather scraps, milk bottle tops and strips of silver foil. These are attached with short dressmaker pins. If adhesive is used with polystyrene it should have a PVA base.

TRAVELLERS THROUGH THE AGES

1460

1580

1140

1640

Figures cut from paper. Decorated with paint,
pastel, chalk or fabric scraps. Extra
decoration added by sticking on sequins,
feathers, buttons, ric-rac, braid and silver
paper scraps.

1780

1870

1970

Draw figure of monk on stiff card. Paint and
decorate. Onto the back of the cut-out firmly
glue a matchbox so that the figure, when
mounted, stands away from the backcloth.

A signboard can be made either by joining two pieces of card as shown in the diagram or be based upon a thin cardboard box. The inn sign can be made by cutting a symbol from a thick piece of card or polystyrene. This is glued in position and the whole sign is painted. The lettering, which many children would find difficult, can be added last. Letters could be cut from large posters which can often be obtained from commercial firms.

NORMAN MANOR HOUSE

Take a box and affix roof as shown in diagram, using strips of sticky paper to hold it in position. Add external details from scraps of balsa wood or card. Cover with paste and paper and paint. Windows are best added when the paint has dried, using sticky paper cut-outs.

TUDOR HOUSE

Take 5 shoe boxes and group as shown in diagram to form the main structure of the house. The sixth box is glued on top of the main group to form the roof support. Cut 4 wedge-shaped pieces of card (7). Glue the short edge to the top of the roof support and the bottom edge to the main structure. Cover with paste and paper strips, paint and decorate.

GEORGIAN HOUSE

Take two boxes of equal size and glue together as shown. On top of these glue two matchboxes to make the chimneys. Between these fold a piece of card to form the roof. Cover with paste and paper strips, paint and decorate.

MODERN HOUSE

Take a box and add a band of corrugated card around the top edge. The card should be slightly above the top edge of the box, forming a roof garden. Cover with paste and paper strips, paint and decorate.

The keep is constructed from three boxes as shown in diagram. The corner towers are made with matchboxes and the crenellations added from cut card. Cover with paste and paper strips, paint and decorate.

A 'see in' keep could be made from seven boxes arranged as shown. Crenellations and details added with card or any appropriate junk material.

Figures in both models are made from clay
and fabric scraps.

Complicated structures such as these churches can be made by selecting boxes and glueing them together. Roofs are made from card. The finished model is covered with paste and paper strips and painted. Windows and fine details made with brightly coloured paper. Trees made with wire and cotton wool dipped in paint. Tombstones made from clay or brick scraps. People made from clay may be added to bring the model to life.

Take a detergent pack and remove the nozzle and seal the opening. Construct sail from thin strips of balsa wood, matchsticks being added to give detail. The door is made from a strip of stiff card. Cover the base with paste and paper strips, and decorate. Paint the sails. When the two units are dry attach the sails, using a brass upholsterers pin.

Take a cardboard tube.
Add a dome shaped ball of clay or Plasticine
to the top of the tube.
Below this add a coil of clay. Cover the whole
model with paste and paper strips.
Glue this to a base (balsa wood or cardboard
box).
Paint and decorate, using clay and fabric
scraps for detail.

VEHICLES THROUGH THE AGES

Top left to right: Roman chariot; a char 1350; on horseback 1400; sedan chair 1665; Royal Mail coach 1784; hobbyhorse 1819.

Below left to right: Omnibus 1830; a penny farthing 1875; hackney cab 1845; Ford Model T 1908; a London bus 1923; car 1970.

A LIFEBOAT HOUSE AND RAMP

Take a box and add a card roof as shown in
diagram. Add a ramp made from card and glue
to the main structure, cover with paste and
paper strips, paint and decorate.

Glue 7 square boxes onto a base of thick card (approx. 12 x 6). The light is fashioned from a piece of Plasticine.

Fix the light to the top of a cardboard tube, pushing the end into another box which has been half filled with sand. This is then mounted as shown in first diagram.

The hull shapes are cut from card and attached to the boxes, the deck being built up with card, paste and paper strips. Paint and decorate. When the paint has dried add mast and superstructure, using any appropriate waste materials which are available.

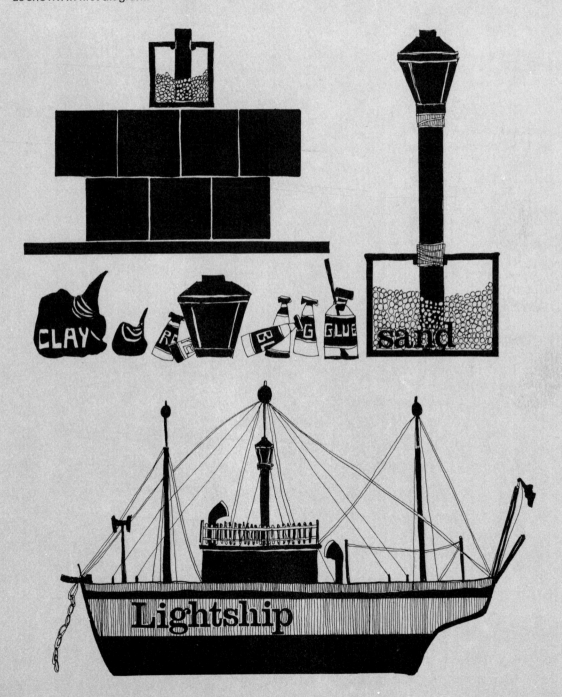

APPENDIX 4

Suppliers of art and craft materials

Paints, papers, brushes
Arnold & Co. Ltd., Butterley Street, Leeds, Yorks
A. Brown, Perth Street, West, Hull, Yorks
Dryad Ltd., Northgates, Leicester
Keep & Sons Ltd., 15 Theobalds Road, London W.C.1
Margros Ltd., Monument Way West, Woking, Surrey
Reeves & Sons Ltd., Lincoln Road, Enfield, Middlesex
Rowney & Co. Ltd., Bracknell New Town, Berkshire
Winsor & Newton Ltd., Wealdstone, Harrow, Middlesex
E.S.A., The Pinnacles, Harlow, Essex

Plasticine
Harbutts Ltd., Bathampton, Bath, Somerset

Synthetic clays
Newclay Ltd., Sunnyfield Road, Chislehurst, Kent

Wax crayons
Cosmic Crayon Co., Ampthill Road, Bedford